MERSEYSIDE'S
OWN

CHRISTINE DAWE

FOREWORD BY FRANK FIELD MP

The
History
Press

To my dearly loved friends and family

The author in the ITV series How We Used To Live.

First published 2012

The History Press
The Mill, Brimscombe Port
Stroud, Gloucestershire, GL5 2QG
www.thehistorypress.co.uk

British Library Cataloguing in Publication Data.
A catalogue record for this book is available from the British Library.

ISBN 978 0 7524 6218 9

Typesetting and origination by The History Press
Printed in Great Britain

Contents

Foreword

By the Right Honourable Frank Field,
Member of Parliament for Birkenhead

Nobody who has read *Liverpool's Own* will be surprised that Christine Dawe is back, as they say, by popular demand. If anything her selection of Merseysiders who have helped build the nation is even more surprising. I say surprising because I had little idea of just how many of the famous of our country have roots in Merseyside, or who have made their names here. Arthur Askey, Sir Thomas Beecham, Dame Rose Heilbron are just a few of the surprises this time.

I would like to concentrate on one person who was born and bred in Liverpool and who was for much of her life the most outstanding back bench member of the House of Commons since William Wilberforce – of anti-slavery campaign fame. I am talking here about Eleanor Rathbone, of course.

The name Rathbone is still well known in Liverpool, but I sometimes wonder whether today's school generation hear much of her great work. It is therefore doubly good to have her presented in *Merseyside's Own*. While, of course, she was in every sense Liverpool's own, Eleanor was owned by a far, far larger audience. This body of world citizens stretched beyond our shores, beyond the darkest corner of Nazi Germany to the far reaches of what was then Imperial India.

Eleanor helped change the financial position of mothers. She fought the subjection of women to the caste system in India. Eleanor was also instrumental in trying to persuade the Allies to make saving the Jews one of the West's war aims. It is to the Allies' eternal shame that they did not do so but, undaunted, Eleanor immediately set about saving as many Jewish children as she could. One of the most moving events that I have ever attended at the House of Commons was a celebration to mark the fiftieth anniversary of her death. Elderly Jewish gentlemen rose to testify how Eleanor had saved them and, by saving each one of them, saved the world for them.

Eleanor was an independent MP – she belonged to no political party. Here perhaps is the reason she isn't better remembered today; there is no political party claiming her as one of their great heroes. But possibly it is because she was a woman, and Britain has a terrible habit of seeing heroes in terms all too often of men. Both *Liverpool's Own* and *Merseyside's Own* show that women have been and are still prepared to make significant use of their talents and dedication to contribute to the welfare of our region and, indeed, to the whole nation. And that too tells us something special about Merseyside.

Introduction

Merseyside has everything anyone could possibly want. Within this region, there is such a wealth of variety, anyone could spend a lifetime inside its boundaries and still see something different every day – from fine, white, sandy beaches, sandhills and pine woods, to a thriving metropolis – from a sixteenth-century hall to a safari park – from potato plantations to numerous huge and elegant parks. Merseyside boasts three professional football clubs, Liverpool, Everton and Tranmere Rovers. There are rugby clubs, golf clubs by the score, riding schools and an international tennis tournament. For industries, take your pick between ship building, glass manufacture, real ale, pharmaceuticals, Jaguar cars and award-winning film and television productions. Miles of docks look out across the sea to Ireland and America and Merseyside's art galleries, theatres and classical concert halls are unrivalled for quality and popularity. As for pop music – need I say more?

Three universities and numerous colleges offer the widest possible choice of subjects. Ask any local student where the best nightclubs and bars are to be found and they will say, 'Look around you.'

Where else would you find two of the finest examples of under-river road tunnels? Passengers on the most luxurious cruise liners in the world admire the superb architecture of the Merseyside waterfront and, 'if you want a cathedral, we've got one to spare!' Of course, none of this came into being overnight. It has taken our ancestors centuries of effort and ingenuity to establish what we now take for granted. But none of the man-made venues could have been created without the existence of the River Mersey itself. This river has flowed out from its wide estuary into the Irish Sea since time immemorial. It has always been the lifeblood of the region. Before man settled in the surrounding countryside, the banks of the Mersey were inhabited by a wide variety of wildlife. Red squirrels, deer, hedgehogs, foxes and sheep wandered freely over the pastures and marshlands. In the fresh waters of nearby springs, streams and lagoons, the variety of fish, geese, ducks and swans was unparalleled, while the beaches lining the foreshore played host to everything from shrimps to dolphins and seals.

When man realised the benefits of life on the banks of this wide and free-flowing river, fishing villages, farms and ferries were created to serve man's needs. A wide diversity of natural resources offered themselves to the growing civilisation. The Romans occupied these shores for 300 years, leaving behind many descendants as well as linguistic and cultural benefits.

Towns, boroughs, holiday resorts and commercial cities gradually evolved. Trade with other countries became of paramount importance, leading, at one stage, to the most dishonourable period in the history of Merseyside. Not only were wealthy merchants involved in the trading triangle connected with slaves, sugar, spices and manufactured goods but they were using their ill-gotten profits for purely selfish advancement. Their employees benefitted little from their own slave-like labours.

A century or so later, when the Irish Potato Famine cast thousands of desperate refugees across the Irish Sea and into Merseyside, the area almost perished under the intolerable death toll from dysentry, cholera and widespread starvation. Those who could, fled. But those who stayed added to the gene pool of the locality. They, along with many other welcome nationalities who chose to integrate with the indigenous citizens of Merseyside, contributed much to the dynamism and humour that now typifies a genuine Scouser and his 'kissing cousins' who live nearby. It is this noble pot-pourri of celebrities that we now celebrate and salute in *Merseyside's Own*.

Cyril Abraham

1919–79

Writer of The Onedin Line *and the man who once did a Beatle's homework*

The sails billow out, the waves crash against the bows and the majestic music echoes the cadences of the breaking surf. In *The Onedin Line*, one of the most popular BBC drama series of all time, the SS *Charlotte Rhodes* leaves the Mersey Estuary and puts to sea once more. Armchair voyagers relax in the knowledge that the next hour will bring storms, rivalry, romance, double-dealing, danger and ultimate success. The fact that an undercurrent of genuine Victorian maritime history gives depth to the narrative, is a welcome bonus.

Set in the years between 1860 and 1886, the saga unfolds. James Onedin (Peter Gilmore) handsome yet stern and unyielding, is an impoverished sea captain. In an astute marriage of convenience, he weds a plain, older woman, Anne Webster (Anne Stallybrass, actually considerably younger than Gilmore). They come to love each other and their deep devotion plays a key role in the development of the first two series. Tragedy strikes when Anne Onedin dies in childbirth, leaving the widowed James free to pursue other romances, culminating in two further marriages in the total of eight series and ninety-one episodes.

Cyril Abraham.

The authenticity of the storylines and the historic exterior locations were highly valued by a discerning public, many of whom were ex-seagoing folk themselves. Every detail was scanned and analysed by loyal fans. Many correspondents wrote to Cyril, the creator and writer of the saga. One erstwhile sea captain claimed that he recognised the ship being used in one programme from his own experiences at sea.

'I remember a certain distinctive scratch on the woodwork. It's been there for as long as I can recall. How wonderful to see the real thing on the ocean again,' he wrote. In actual fact, the interior of the 'ship' was a plywood set, constructed within the shell of an ex-church building, St Peter's in Dickinson Road, Manchester. This makeshift studio was used for many drama productions as well as for quiz shows such as *Call My Bluff*.

The River Mersey, too was a sham. The real docks and harbour board at Birkenhead and Liverpool were now so modern, with cranes and containers visible everywhere, a substitute had to be found. Exeter and Dartmouth still retained the quaint old-fashioned appeal of bygone times, while the Welsh shorelines around Pembroke doubled convincingly for nineteenth-century Turkey and Portugal. Khachaturian's resounding music for the ballet, *Spartacus*, added to the atmospheric opening titles. The acclaimed acting skills of a perfectly matched cast ensured *The Onedin Line*'s place in the list of top television period dramas of all time.

'How did you get started in writing?', 'What did you do before?' and 'Where do you get your ideas?' are the three most frequently asked questions to all authors and scriptwriters.

Before success came his way, Cyril Abraham was a Liverpool bus driver with literary ambitions. Before that he had been a Marconi wireless operator in the Merchant Navy, on ships transporting food and essential medical supplies during the Second World War. He was lucky enough to escape unscathed despite some alarming encounters in dangerous waters. Then came a spell as a 'Bevin Boy' down the mines at Bold Colliery. As a youth, he had trained at HMS *Conway* and before that he was a pupil at the Liverpool Collegiate. But the end of the war saw him at a loose end, not sure what to make of the rest of his life. As a temporary measure he joined Liverpool City Transport. At Smithdown Road bus depot, his driving instructor was Harry Harrison, a friendly man who was often ready to chat about his own life when at sea with the White Star Line. One day he said to Cyril, 'I'm fed up with my teenage lay-about son. He doesn't concentrate in school, he doesn't do his homework and he's got in with some useless gang of lads. All they do is hang around messing with guitars and drums. What use is that? How's he going to earn a living like that?' On another occasion, Harry came to Cyril with a school exercise book in his hand.

'Cyril,' he said, 'You're an educated feller. My youngest is at the Institute but he can't do this homework. And I can't make it out either. Will you have a go at it – and our kid can copy it out in his own handwriting later.' Cyril duly obliged and there were other occasions when he was glad to help, too.

It was some years later when Cyril bumped into Harry again. When he did pass him in the street, Cyril spoke with tongue in cheek.

'Hello Harry, how's that no-good son of yours these days?' Harry took it all in good humour and replied, 'Oh, the other day he said to me, "You've always liked the horses, haven't you Dad? Well here's your birthday present. It's the credentials for a pedigree race horse. He'll be stabled and trained for you. You're registered as the owner."'

Peter Gilmore, star of The Onedin Line.

'So you're proud of George now that he's one of the Fab Four, then?' smiled Cyril and they both had a good laugh.

It was at about this time that Cyril met Joan, a Liverpool teacher. Now Cyril's widow, Joan takes up the sequence of events:

> I thought he seemed an interesting sort of chap, so I asked him what he did for a living. When he told me about his various occupations, he added that he really wanted to become a writer. 'Why don't you then?' I asked.
>
> 'Well I can't afford a typewriter and no editors or agents will look at anything in handwriting,' was his excuse. So I went into the city centre and looked in the window of an office supply shop. There was a notice saying, SALE – TYPEWRITERS – FOUR GUINEAS. It was the end of the month so I had hardly any cash left from my salary but I went in anyway. When I asked about the sale, the assistant said, 'Yes, madam. Just those over there.'
>
> 'But they're a hideous shade of bright pink!'
>
> 'Yes, madam. That's why they're reduced. No offices want pink typewriters.'
>
> 'Well, I haven't got four guineas on me, anyway,' I said.
>
> 'We have hire purchase facilities. It's half-a-crown down and half-a-crown per week.'
>
> So I scraped up what coins I had in my purse and gave him 5s for the first two payments. And I had to pay out some more, for ribbons, of course.

She took the typewriter to Cyril's home and gave it to him. A week later, she asked him if he'd written anything yet.

'I can't,' he said. 'I can't afford any paper.'

They had a friend who worked in an office. Before the days of recycling, secretaries frequently used to throw away unused sheets of paper. So each night, Joan's friend went around all the offices in her building, found any unwanted paper and brought it home for Cyril. At last he had no excuse, so he started work. He began with short stories and articles, some of which were accepted by Australian magazines. When Cyril submitted a screenplay to the BBC, he was invited to meet Andrew Osborne in a London restaurant. He said that Cyril's script was just what he was looking for.

'I've had too many plays where the characters are just cardboard cut-outs,' he said. 'Your people have got real ROOTS !' As he boomed out ROOTS, he thumped the table so hard that all the cutlery jumped up into the air then clattered onto the floor. The waiter hurried over thinking that the two men were having a row.

After contracts were signed, two high-ranking BBC executives rang Cyril to say that they were in Manchester and could they meet up? Cyril invited them to his father's bungalow in Manley between Frodsham and Delamere Forest. Joan provided all the ingredients for a special gourmet lunch but couldn't stay, as she was teaching. Cyril took the two producers for a business stroll through the beautiful National Trust forest. On their return, Cyril asked his father if he had cooked the meal.

'Oh yes,' was the reply. 'It was delicious. I ate most of it and gave the left-overs to the dog.' The two producers didn't get a bite to eat – the only bite they did get was on the ankle, from the ungrateful dog. Cyril had to take them to the nearby Goshawke Pub for a liquid lunch.

Fortunately, the programmes became so successful that all was forgiven. After the series finished, Cyril then adapted the saga of the Onedin family into novels. These were translated into many different languages, the television programmes were sold all over the world and the novels became the basis for audiobooks recorded by Ulverscroft Isis Soundings and voiced by Ray Dunbobbin. When Cyril was earning four- and five-figure fees per weekly episode, his father warned him not to be rash.

'It won't last,' he said, 'I think you should go back to the buses. It's a steady wage, with a pension and a smart uniform provided. Can the BBC match that?'

After their marriage, Joan and Cyril moved into the secluded bungalow, a converted cricket pavilion, in Manley. Liver failure, exacerbated by a fondness for alcohol, caused Cyril's early death in 1979 but his radio plays, books and the repeats of his television programmes are a constant testament to his innate talent as a raconteur and the value of a hideous pink typewriter.

Jean Alexander

Hilda Ogden, Aunty Wainwright and a host of others

'Stanley! I want a huge Muriel of a landscape to cover the whole of this wall!'
'Oh aye? And I s'pose yer want a flight of plastic ducks flyin' across it, an all?'
'Oo, yeah. That 'ud be just pairfect. Plaster ducks an' a Muriel. We'll 'ave both.'
Hilda and Stan Ogden, in *Coronation Street*

In her autobiography, *The Other Side of the Street*, Jean writes that many people have asked her, 'Who were you before you were Hilda Ogden?'

'It is true,' she comments, 'that *Coronation Street* took up a third of my life but there was a Jean Alexander before I ever stepped into the Granada Studios and there is still a Jean Alexander since I left the programme.'

Jean was born in Toxteth, in the area where all the streets have Welsh names. She went to Granby Street School and later to St Edmund's College. She owes her love of literature to her English Mistress, Miss Potter, 'A brilliant teacher who had me hooked on Shakespeare by the age of fourteen.' But Jean's fascination with show business in general began even earlier, in a lodging house in Barrow-in-Furness. Jean's father was working at

the shipyard for a few months, so the close-knit family moved with him. Staying at the same boarding house was a dance troupe of about a dozen girls. Little Jean watched them rehearse in the backyard and then tried to copy their steps.

'Some of the glamour which covered them like stardust,' she says, 'worked its way into my young heart and stayed there, hidden like a seed that is going to flower in some distant spring.'

During the Second World War, Jean was at first evacuated to Chester but this turned out to be potentially no safer than Liverpool, due to its proximity to Sealand Aerodrome where RAF pilots were trained. Sailors awaiting embarkation in Liverpool were also wandering around everywhere in Chester, so Jean soon returned home. Living at that time in a house with a cellar, used as a makeshift air-raid shelter, Jean's pet kitten frequently acted as an air-raid early warning system. Several minutes before any siren sounded, a startled Snooky would jump up from his favourite cushion by the fire and scurry

downstairs to hide under the camp bed. Sure enough, a bombing raid would always follow. Obviously Snooky had super-sensitive hearing and could accurately detect the sound of enemy aircraft even at a great distance. The family gratefully followed him, often with half-eaten meals in their hands.

In 1944, Jean went to work for the Liverpool Library Service but her acting ambitions were struggling to find an outlet. After several brief theatrical appearances and some non-acting jobs, such as wardrobe mistress at Oldham Rep, where one of the giant baskets containing costumes turned out to be also the nesting place of a huge, gingery coloured rat, Jean eventually received an invitation from Donald Bodley to join the Southport Repertory Theatre, 'Just for a single week's production only,' he told her. The play, *See How They Run*, a popular and hilarious farce, was such a success that Jean was granted just one more week's engagement. Seven years later, Jean was still a member of the company, having played every conceivable character in a vast variety of tragedies, comedies and classical plays. Southport had much to recommend it and Jean has enjoyed living there ever since. Then came one of Jean's favourite periods of her career, five years at the Theatre Royal, York, where she still has friends. A short season at the Liverpool Playhouse Theatre gave her the pleasure of working with director Willard Stoker and actors Benjamin Whitrow, Caroline Blakiston and Rita Tushingham. In total, Jean had twelve years of theatre and film experience before her first appearance in *Coronation Street*.

Jean recalls with great affection her many years working with Bernard Youens, her 'husband', Stan, in *Coronation Street*. Her fond pet name for him was 'Bunny'.

'Our rapport was obvious from the outset,' she says. They became the perfect colleagues. 'Our method was to know the lines thoroughly, play around with them to make the very best of the script. Then go to a quiet corner to rehearse together while, at the same time, playing Scrabble and swearing vehemently if the other one made a clever move.'

'Hilda' always had a twinkle in her eye and such was the warmth and humour that Jean brought to her pinny-and-curler-wearing alter ego, the nation took her to their hearts. In a 1982 poll, the public voted that the most recognisable women in Britain were Queen Elizabeth II, the Queen Mother, Princess Diana and Hilda Ogden. In the 1980s, for *four* consecutive years Jean won the TV Times Best Actress Award and, in 1985, the Royal TV Society Best Performance. In 1987 she received Radio Merseyside's Scouseology Trophy For Lifetime Achievement. The gossipy nosey-parker whose conversations were decorated with many endearing Malapropisms enlivened and enriched Corrie for twenty-three years. Sir Laurence Olivier adored her and formed the Hilda Ogden Appreciation Society, recruiting many other famous fans.

Jean has the capacity to learn new dialogue every day, no matter how tricky the vocabulary. Other cast members, however, often stumbled over their lines. One such was Margot Bryant, better remembered as Minnie Caldwell. She would often waffle with her words, substituting lines that the script-writers had never written, such as 'My father had a big dog once. It was a ferret.'

When Jean finally decided to shake the past out of Hilda's dusters, twenty million viewers shed a little tear at her farewell party in The Rover's Return.

As Hilda Ogden moved away from Weatherfield, Jean Alexander found a fresh and highly successful phase in her career. At the BBC, the advent of Aunty Wainwright and her Aladdin's cave of bric-a-brac breathed new life into the long-running *Last of the Summer Wine*. As cunning as the Artful Dodger, with her dubious deals, this devious old dear must surely have kissed the Blarney Stone. Once again, Jean invested the character with an underlying warmth that endeared her to viewers and kept them chuckling at all her wily little scams for more than twenty years. Jean now regards 'Aunty' as 'my favourite role ever!' What a happy and satisfying thing to be able to say.

Arthur Askey CBE
1900–82

'Big-Hearted Arthur, they call me!'

Does it still exist? That old-fashioned wooden desk that once graced a classroom in the Liverpool Institute Grammar School for Boys, now the Liverpool Institute for the Performing Arts? That desk where the young Paul McCartney once sat and, by chance, noticed the carved name of a former famous pupil, Arthur Bowden Askey? Was it naughty vandalism or the creation of a show-biz relic with these two such celebrated associations? And where is it now?

Arthur Askey was born at 39 Moses Street, at the turn of the twentieth century. His father worked in the office of a firm with long connections to the importing of sugar from the West Indies. Arthur's mother originally came from Knutsford, Cheshire, the real location of *Cranford* by Mrs Gaskell, filmed as a serial by the BBC.

Arthur's accent was never of a true Scouse intonation but a tone unique to himself. Years of being the youthful lead in Isle of Wight concert parties may have influenced this popular comedian's pronunciation, turning his catchphrase, 'I thank you,' into 'Aye thang yeow,'

and making 'Beefore your VERRIE eyes,' and 'Hello Pliymates,' sound almost cockney in their wide-mouthed exuberance.

As a youngster, Arthur's clear singing voice earned him parts in school concerts and a place in the church choir at St Michael-in-the-Hamlet. After leaving the Institute, he became a clerical assistant in the Education Department of the Liverpool City Council. In spite of poor vision, he was called up into the army towards the end of the First World War where he spent most of his time in Entertainments, keeping up morale and dispelling boredom. His popularity grew with every show.

Having natural charisma and immense vitality, he accentuated his humorous appearance with 'Harry Potter'-style, black-rimmed glasses. He often sported a trilby hat, several sizes too small, emphasising his unusually large head and long chin on his diminutive body.

His dapper appearance and sparkling personality were ideal for silly jokes, silly songs and even sillier dances, all apparently childishly innocent but cunningly interspersed with saucy little *double-entendres*. During the Second World War, his satirical song, 'It's Really Nice to See you, Mr Hess', and the patriotic 'We're Going to hang out the Washing on the Siegfried Line', caused him to be included in a Nazi hit-list, condemning him to be shot if the Germans ever invaded Britain!

After years touring with concert parties and pantomimes, radio beckoned and Arthur teamed up with Richard Murdoch in a programme called *Band Wagon*. Richard – tall, elegant and urbane – was the perfect foil for cheeky little Arthur. The original scripts for *Band Wagon* were weak and boring, so Arthur and 'Stinker' Murdoch wrote their own, vastly funnier material. This eventually led to the crazy comedy in which the two supposedly shared a flat at the top of Broadcasting House. As this was radio, other characters could be anything from talking pigeons and a goat to a girl named Nausea and her mother, Mrs Bagwash.

Television was the next step. Arthur was a natural. His timing and facial expressions were faultless and, talking straight to camera, he endeared himself to even wider audiences. When interviewed and asked if he had to find new jokes for television, his candid admission, 'No, I just rearrange them into a different order!' was delivered with such an engaging twinkle, it became a joke in itself.

In real life, too, he was always warm and friendly. His marriage was happy. He and his wife, Elizabeth, had one daughter, Anthea, who eventually became an actress.

During the 1970s, the talent show *New Faces*, hosted by Mickie Most and song writer Tony Hatch, also included the kindly, big-hearted Arthur. He was the 'nice' one who always had an encouraging word for the hopefuls.

Several films including *Charlie's Aunt* and *The Ghost Train*, completed Arthur's long catalogue of every form of entertainment, prompting pop producer Pete Waterman to buy the rights to every one of Askey's films.

After his final film, *Night Nurse*, ill health forced Arthur to retire. Eventually, circulatory problems necessitated the amputation of both legs. Even at the age of eighty-two, his popularity had not waned. Succeeding generations of comedians were still learning from his wide-ranging successes. His name lives on as one of the most endearing and enduring personalities of the Liverpool comedy scene.

Dame Beryl Bainbridge
1932/33/34(?)–2010

Actress, author – 'the Booker Bridesmaid'

The actual date of Beryl Bainbridge's birth is, fittingly for the author of such strange and perplexing fiction, shrouded in mystery – but not so the rest of her life, as many of her early novels draw upon her personal experiences, her childhood, her various employments and her emotional entanglements.

The most important fact about her is her unique talent and style of prose. Eighteen books, many weirdly humorous novels and a handful of historical chronicles brought her plaudits and prizes, including the Guardian Literary Prize and the Whitbread Award, although the Man Booker Prize continually eluded her. In spite of five of her books being nominated over a period of years, she never actually won the Booker Prize, a reminder of the phrase, 'Always a bridesmaid, never the bride.' Accustomed from an early age to disappointments and frustrations, Beryl bore the results stoically, comforted by nicotine and alcohol. At parties, she was famous for her heavy smoking, drinking and falling over.

Born in Liverpool and raised in Formby, Merseyside, by her fretful mother and unpredictable father, little Beryl and her brother, Ian, had to cope with a home saturated with screaming quarrels followed by resentful silences. Their salesman father's income was adequate, if somewhat questionable in origins. He had gone bankrupt before Beryl was born but could afford golf clubs and excellent educational opportunities for his children. Without explanation, he often persuaded his little daughter to sign cheques in her name. Beryl and Ian were both sent to the prestigious Merchant Taylors' School in nearby Waterloo. Beryl had private Elocution, Music, Latin and Tap Dancing lessons. Her high-pitched and precise pronunciation won her an *ingénue* role in the BBC Radio programme *Children's Hour*, with Billie Whitelaw and Judith Chalmers. In spite of her father's appreciation of her talents, Beryl hated his frightening threats and violent outbursts. Even though the house had four bedrooms, Beryl and her mother slept in one room and Ian and Mr Bainbridge shared another. Before she was ten, Beryl was dreaming of ways to kill her father.

As an adult, Beryl claimed that the only reason she started writing was to 'make sense of what went on it my past . . . from a writer's point of view, it was an ideal childhood. I've never really written fiction. What would be the point? What is more peculiar, devious and horrific than real life?'

Of course, the teenage Beryl's personality was badly affected by so much turmoil at home. She was always fighting at school, earning the nickname of 'Basher' Bainbridge. When a classmate showed her a 'dirty rhyme', giggling, Beryl scribbled an equally rude cartoon and slipped it into her gymslip pocket. Her mother discovered this and indignantly took it to the Head at Merchant Taylors'. Beryl was blamed as a 'corrupting influence' and immediately expelled. She was sent away to the Cone-Ripman School in Tring, Hertfordshire, now called Tring Park School for the Performing Arts. This gave Beryl the opportunity to express herself in Art, English and History. But she left at sixteen with no qualifications.

Back in Merseyside, near the Southport beaches, Beryl met a German ex-prisoner of war. She and Harry Franz fell in love and had secret trysts 'night after night' in the pine

woods and sand dunes along the local coastline, until Harry was suddenly repatriated to his homeland. For six years both tried to obtain permits for Harry to return to Britain, all to no avail. Eventually, they had to admit defeat and their contact faded away.

Beryl's father, still helping her educationally, if not emotionally, managed to find her a position as assistant stage manager at the Liverpool Playhouse. This led to small acting parts and enough back-stage experience to inspire *An Awfully Big Adventure* (a name inspired by Peter Pan's thoughts on death) about an innocent teenage actress embroiled in a questionable relationship with an older man (Alan Rickman and Hugh Grant starred in the 1989 film version of this novel). Beryl's short acting career also brought her a minor character in a few episodes of *Coronation Street*.

Beryl's early work, *Harriet Said*, failed to find a publisher for many years, due to the fact that the thirteen-year-old anti-heroine had 'an evil mind . . . repulsive beyond belief!' All Ms Bainbridge's novels are tense, bleak and menacing. Yet, as with ancient Greek tragedies, there are flashes of humour, even farcical moments. Every book, including her later historical novels, end with violent or tragic death. She admitted that she had been preoccupied with death from childhood, partly influenced by cinema newsreels of wartime concentration camps. Captain Scott's monumental attempt to reach the South Pole fascinated her, partly because of the numerous lives it cost. Her book *The Birthday Boys* recalled the saga. The *Titanic* provided the theme for *Every Man For Himself*, quoting Captain Smith's final instructions.

In 1954, (aged either twenty, twenty-one or twenty-two), she married Austin Davies, the resident set-designer and artist at the Liverpool Playhouse. After the births of their son and daughter in 1957 and 1958, Austin had an affair and abandoned Beryl to bring up the children alone. Beryl was tempted to commit suicide but, oddly, the separation inspired more writing. She embraced the bohemian lifestyle of an actress/author, ignoring passing fashions and dressing in her own style. She smoked and drank excessively, collapsed at parties, then tried to become Jewish – 'but they wouldn't have me,' so she converted to Catholicism, filling her home with religious statues, Victorian pictures and ultimately, a huge stuffed buffalo called Eric.

In the early 1960s, Beryl's ex-husband returned and bought a house for her and the children in Albert Street, Camden Town. He then rented the basement flat as her tenant, an arrangement that lasted until he eventually remarried and emigrated to New Zealand. Fact is stranger than even Beryl's fiction. One day, Austin's ageing mother turned up at Beryl's front door, with a gun in her hand, shot wildly but fortunately missed Beryl, who used the incident in her book, *The Bottle Factory Outing* which won her the Guardian Fiction Prize. The whole story was rooted in fact, as the author worked part-time labelling wine bottles in a nearby factory.

Beryl's affair with the writer Alan Sharp, brought her a third child, a daughter. The relationship ended in true Bainbridge style when Alan went out to fetch something from his car and, like Captain Oates in her book *The Birthday Boys*, never came back. Even when dealing with dramatic crises such as Scott's fatal expedition to the Antarctic, Bainbridge was still haunted by the spectre of her father's violent personality in spite of the fact that, as she says, 'Scott went to the South Pole and my father never went further than the corner shop.'

In contrast to her own upbringing, Beryl strove to be an affectionate and supportive mother and grandmother. As lung cancer began taking its toll on her health, her grandson, Charlie Russell, filmed a documentary for the BBC, calling it *Beryl's Last Year*.

In spite of shaky beginnings, Beryl's work was at last recognised for its true originality and pithy brilliance. In 2000, she was appointed Dame Commander of the British Empire, was honoured with a Doctor of Literature Degree by Liverpool University and in 2011 was recognised posthumously with a Booker Prize.

Hugh Baird
1908–82

So good they named a college after him

Hugh Baird is remembered in the local press as 'Bootle's Man of Vision' and the 'Caring Politician'. His contribution to the area's education, its transport system and its commerce is revered and honoured by the name of Bootle's vibrant and highly successful college of education, the Hugh Baird College. His portrait joins other civic dignitaries of Bootle on the walls of the Town Hall. The original National Girobank owes its existence to his insight and tenacity. Alderman Hugh Baird was first elected to the Bootle Council in 1941 and, except for a two-year gap between 1945 and 1947, he served continuously on the council until 1974. The highlight of his career came in 1959/60 when he took office as the Mayor of Bootle.

This constitutes an interesting and laudable vocation for one who had had to leave school as soon as he was thirteen and who, at the age of eighteen, was imprisoned after being found guilty of mutiny on the high seas. What is more, in later life, his twenty-eight day incarceration was viewed with a sense of pride by this man of honour and devotion to duty.

After his early farewell to Balliol School, young Hugh started work at Bootle Docks. The conditions were harsh and extremely poorly paid. The day started at six and continued for long, back-breaking hours until the sun set on the Sefton horizon. Unemployment was so widespread that any job, however gruelling, was seen as a bonus. Like many other Merseyside youngsters, Hugh saw a possible escape by becoming a sea-going man. After two years as an apprentice docker, he joined the Merchant Navy. A wider experience of

Hugh Baird with boys bound for the British India educational cruise ship SS Nevasa.

the world opened up to him but the work was just as hard and almost as poorly paid. And things went from bad to worse. While he was serving on the *Cornwall* the navy actually *reduced* wages. Even as a teenager, Hugh had determined views on justice and the rights of labourers. Having, in those days, no strong union to fight on their behalf, Hugh and twenty others decided to strike. But the powers-that-be were all powerful. All twenty-one were charged, found guilty and sent down for a calendar month. Hugh's days at sea were over and the docks were the only avenue open to him, until eventually he managed to find work driving a tram in Liverpool.

Just as he was beginning to take a more active interest in local government, the Second World War broke out. His past misdemeanours were forgotten and he was seen as a suitable candidate for the Royal Navy. Glad to defend his homeland, Hugh was prepared to suffer along with his fellow countrymen on the perilous seas around Europe. But at least part of his service was spent as a driver attached to the local destroyer depot. This was no 'cushy number' as Bootle was under constant threat from the relentless bombing by enemy planes. The docks were the prime target but the whole area was torn asunder. The locality was all but annihilated and civilian casualties were heart-rendingly high. Every day, every night, everyone in the neighbourhood took their lives in their hands whether they ventured out or stayed at home.

After the war, Hugh's interest in local government increased. As he never married, he was not constrained by family commitments so he was able to devote all his time and energy to civic duties. Influenced by his own early experiences, his two main concerns were education and transport. He became chairman of the Transport Committee and also of the Bootle Education Committee. As well as improving the roads and bus routes, Hugh became the manager of St Oswald's Church of England School and of St Robert Bellarmine Roman Catholic School. He always attended every important educational conference. He was delighted that so many new schools were built in the Netherton area but what was more important to him was the quality of the teaching within those buildings. He wrote a newspaper article stating that he hoped, 'The opportunity is now seized of making the subjects taught in schools relevant to the time in which children live. The new school child must leave school as an adult ready for the adult world.' His utopian dream was to have 'a school on almost every street corner.' He advocated foreign trips to learn about other countries and he also hoped that future generations of parents would encourage their children to remain in education for longer than he had been able to.

Elected unanimously as Bootle's Mayor in 1959, his Lady Mayoress was Councillor Mrs Bray who 'had done invaluable work as Chair of the Children's Committee, as well as the Jim Becket Club for Old People, and had won the respect of young and old alike.'

Hugh used his year in office to concern himself with every possible aspect of the borough. From the Sea Cadets and the Maple Leaf Boxing Club to the local sewers, he was there making sure that everything was in order and that everyone felt that his or her contribution to Bootle was valued. Equally at home in any company, he welcomed Princess Margaret on her visit to the North, pleased at the publicity this could bring to his home town.

Due to advances in technology at the Merseyside docks, machinery was taking over jobs traditionally assigned to the work force. The prosperity of the region had been sadly lacking for years. Unemployment became an ugly scourge and those who could, started to move away. In 1968, when the Labour Government under Harold Wilson put forward plans to inaugurate a National Girobank to speed up payments of salaries and transfers of fees, Councillor Baird grasped an opportunity. He was instrumental in persuading Tony Benn, the then Postmaster General, to choose the site in Bootle of a disused railway siding. After much negotiation, employment was provided for local builders and craftsmen to create the state-of-the-art premises. The machinery and technology was innovative and impressive. It was the first financial institution in Europe to be established fully computerised from the outset.

Hugh Baird with Princess Margaret.

A new kind of employment came to Bootle and the younger generations were now encouraged to learn different skills. Information technology was eventually introduced into all school and college timetables. Over three decades or more, the Girobank went through several metamorphoses, with a severe dip in the twenty-first century when its future, as part of the Alliance & Leicester group, looked bleak. However, in 2010, Santander took control, and in 2011 optimism soared when Santander brought 100 new jobs into the now commercial banking headquarters in Bridle Road.

When the original Victorian buildings comprising the arts and further educational colleges in Bootle were no longer adequate for the younger population, a new purpose-built college was proposed. As chairman of the Education Committee, Councillor Baird was involved in the planning and creation, right from the start. On its completion in 1974 as a college of further education, the committee and council decided to acknowledge Hugh Baird's commitment to scholarship and culture in the area by naming the establishment in his honour. Over the years, the building was extended and new subjects offered to prospective students. Today, it is considered to be the best further education college on Merseyside, committed to improving life and employment prospects for over 6,000 young people. There are more than 300 courses available, ranging from Business Studies to Bricklaying and from Performing Arts to Public Services such as Police and Fire Brigade. There are part-time or full-time Diplomas, NVQs, A-Levels and Full Honours Degrees, all with admirably high pass-rates. Apprenticeships are also offered to students drawn from schools right across the region. It is a vibrant environment, buzzing with aspirations and expectations.

Hugh Baird would be justly proud of what has been achieved by the dedicated staff and governing body in his name.

Tom Baker

The fourth and longest-serving Doctor Who

A vow of silence and unquestioning self-denial. Six years of self-effacing modesty, gazing always downwards, rising before dawn for devotional prayer even in mid-winter, pledging oneself to poverty, abstinence and demeaning hard labour. For someone with a wicked sense of humour, a richly mellifluous voice, natural eloquence, undeniable good looks and childhood fantasies of being a murderer, the solitary life of a monk would seem to be an odd choice. Not only that, but this once-cloistered recluse is now famous in at least seventy-four countries around the world. More than that, at one period in his life he was propositioned by countless female admirers and he confesses to capitulating to some of them.

The storylines of the many series of *Doctor Who* on BBC Television have always featured implausible fantasies of metamorphosis, transforming one illusion into something incredibly different. Tom Baker, this very real human being, has had several improbable transformations himself. It would be interesting to see computer images depicting Tom's progress, from mixed-up Scouse schoolboy during the Second World War, to monk, then soldier, student, actor, television icon, thrice married husband and father, voice-over artist and back to private individual, now fond of a bit of quiet gardening.

Thomas Stewart Baker was born in the area of Liverpool where the districts of West Derby, L12 and Croxteth, L11 almost overlap. His mother was an Irish Catholic and his father was a Jewish seafarer. Money was always in very short supply, so Mrs Baker combined an evening job as a barmaid in the nearby Sefton Arms pub with daytime chores of scrubbing other people's floors.

Although he loved his parents dearly, as he states in his autobiography, wittily entitled *Who on Earth is Tom Baker?*, young Tommy once admitted to his school teacher that his ambition was to be an orphan, because children whose parents died in the Liverpool Blitz received sweets, chewing gum, comics and fashionable clothes from the USA. As he could never think of any real sins to confess to his parish priest, Tommy copied his pal's idea of making up something suitable. It began with little indiscretions such as looking at his mother with a cheeky expression, progressing to impure thoughts (although he had no idea what that meant) and moving blithely on to three murders in one week. The priest was obviously taken aback by this and enquired if the victims were anyone local.

'No, Father, they were all from St Teresa's.'

'Oh, well that's alright then. Remember that Jesus loves you and stay away from St Teresa's.'

Recycling was one of his childhood war efforts. He thought cornflake boxes had to be collected because the RAF dropped bombs made of cardboard on the enemy. He and a friend collected the most waste paper, so they received a certificate from the Lord Mayor, Lord Sefton. Their headmistress was given a pound note, so she treated the boys to lunch at the fashionable Cooper's Café, a film at the Hippodrome, tea at the Kardomah and still had enough left over to give them each ten pence to take home. Tom says, 'That was the only award I have ever won!'

He left school at fifteen and joined a monastic order on Jersey in the Channel Islands. During his six years there, he experienced a confined, inhibiting and restrictive lifestyle. Initially, he felt that this was right for him – he relished the ordeal of self-denigration and worthlessness constantly indoctrinated into him at school. Eventually, he realised that his religious aspirations were an illusion and spiritual healing was not for him. His next incarnation was concerned with physical healing. He joined the Royal Army Medical Corps only to discover that he was still performing menial tasks which were equally as degrading as those at the monastery. As a hobby, he joined the army drama group and immediately discovered a love of acting. His talent for amusing people soon became apparent and the promise of a satisfying career at last entered his life. He won a scholarship to the Rose Bruford School of Speech and Drama, in Kent.

Happiness seemed to come his way when he met and married Anna Wheatcroft, niece of the famous rose grower. Tom and Anna then had two sons but the Wheatcroft family made the unknown young actor feel worthless in comparison to their wealth. They were control freaks, and tried to take Tom's sons away from him. All his old anxieties returned and he attempted suicide. He was even driven to making a vicious physical attack on his mother-in-law, after which he relinquished all connection with the family and returned to acting. Many years later, his now grown-up son once made contact with him in New Zealand.

Several excellent theatrical roles came his way when he was accepted by the National Theatre. Later, he landed the melodramatic role of Rasputin in the television production of *Nicholas and Alexandra*. For this he was nominated in two categories, Best Newcomer and Best Supporting Actor. Shakespearian and Dickensian roles followed but, at the time of his auditions for *Doctor Who*, he was working as a labourer on a building site.

His time as a Time Lord spanned seven years, making him the longest-serving Doctor Who to date. Tom's Doctor Who had several different assistants during the series, including Liverpool-born Elisabeth Sladen. Elisabeth's own spin-off series *The Sarah Jane Adventures* came to the small screens in 2007, but sadly she died in 2011. In real life, Tom married his fifth 'companion' Romana, played by Lalla Ward, but the marriage lasted only sixteen months. In addition to Tom's own charismatic portrayal of the fourth Doctor, his long scarf and the cleverly named robot dog K9, brought him worldwide fame and fortune. Another happy souvenir of Gallifrey was Tom's third and lasting marriage to the beautiful script editor, Sue Jerrard.

As well as many satisfying and highly acclaimed theatrical roles, including a partnership with Liverpool actress Kate Fitzgerald in Willy Russell's *Educating Rita*, Tom won new fans for his television portrayals of the professor in *Medics* with Sue Johnston, and as Donald MacDonald in *Monarch of the Glen*. Then along came *Little Britain* for which he provides the fruity voice-over. His amused comment on this is that 'I'm now being employed by the children who used to watch me as the Doctor!'

Asked for his reaction to having a star named after him, he quipped, 'I'm over the moon!'

Sir Thomas Beecham

1879–1961

Conductor and creator of classical orchestras

'Madam, you have, between your legs, a most beautiful instrument, capable of giving pleasure to many – and all you can do, is scratch it!'

Sir Thomas Beecham, to a lady cellist, at one of his orchestral rehearsals

Born in St Helens, now part of Merseyside but at that time still a small town in rural Lancashire, 'Tommy' Beecham had the lively personality, amazing charisma, ready wit and abundant energy of a true Lancastrian. Proud of his Northern heritage, he would claim, 'In *MY* county, where *I* come from, we're all a bit vulgar, you know, but there is a certain heartiness – a sort of bonhomie about our vulgarity – that tides you over a lot of rough spots.' On being invited to direct at the 1951 Liverpool Festival, he insisted on a fee of nothing but one large Simnel cake and two dozen Eccles cakes. He was paid as requested.

His musical ability and knowledge was outstanding, even from a very early age. He also had a prodigious memory. As a young child he could quote huge swathes of Shakespearian speeches and, in fact, sometimes whole plays.

Tommy's paternal grandfather, also called Thomas, had founded the famous 'Beecham's Little Liver Pills' pharmaceutical company. These pills were highly effective laxatives, greatly esteemed by the late Victorians. They were produced at Mr Beecham Senior's factory in Westfield Street, St Helens. The building now forms part of St Helens Technical College although the ornate reception area and elegant staircase are preserved intact. Mr Beecham and his wife and children lived next door to the business. Their eldest son, Joseph, who also worked for the firm, married a sensitive girl called Josephine and

eventually became Mayor of St Helens. They had ten children, two of whom died in infancy. The eldest surviving was Emily and, four years her junior, came Thomas, their eldest son.

In an era before radio, television or recordings of any sort, Joseph Beecham indulged his own passion for music by collecting vast numbers of musical boxes of all shapes, sizes and designs. These, with the family piano and the local brass bands were, at first, little Tommy's only access to music. Unfortunately, as a baby, he hated brass bands and would scream and cry if one passed by the house. As an adult, he remarked, 'Brass bands are all very well in their place – out of doors and a long distance away.' In subsequent years, with the increasing prosperity of the business, Joseph could easily afford to take his wife and young children in the family carriage on the 'long' journey to Liverpool to visit the opera. Young Tommy immediately began a lifelong love affair with opera and later frequently conducted many of the popular romantic and tragic operas of the day.

Thanks to soaring sales, more space was needed at the factory so the family home was knocked down to facilitate expansion of the business and the Beechams moved to a huge house in Huyton, in those days a leafy village outside Liverpool. Family holidays became more adventurous. Southport was abandoned in favour of a variety of European cultural cities. Business trips to set up a factory in America were also undertaken.

Thomas set his heart on a musical education but his father insisted that he should go to Oxford and then join the flourishing firm. Eventually, after persuading his father to allow him to leave Oxford, Thomas did study Music with Frederic Austin in Liverpool, Charles Wood in London and Moritz Moszkowski in Paris. While still a student, it was at his father's theatrically grand inauguration as Mayor of St Helens that Tommy first conducted an orchestra in public. As well as a sumptuous banquet, the Hallé Orchestra was engaged and paid for by Joseph Beecham. At the last moment, their famous conductor, Dr Hans Richter was unable to attend. With only one very brief rehearsal with the musicians – and none at all with the American soprano soloist, Lillian Blauvelt – Thomas stepped into the breach and successfully added to the impressively flamboyant occasion. Emily missed these celebrations as she was studying Medicine in the United States so Joseph chose his eighteen-year-old daughter Josie, to be his Lady Mayoress. Mrs Beecham did not enjoy the best of health and was deemed too delicate to undertake the civic duties involved.

As well as physical frailties, in middle-age Mrs Josephine Beecham suffered from depression and other psychological problems. Her husband, blinded by wealth and his own importance in society, had no patience for such weakness. Indeed he may have contributed to it, partly due to his own insensitive behaviour and also by not finding suitable treatment for her condition. Without a word to his children, he secretly had his wife committed to a lunatic asylum. When Thomas and his sister, Emily, discovered what had happened, they were furious. With difficulty, they tracked down the place of their mother's incarceration in Northampton. On legal advice they found that she could only be released if she were to divorce Joseph, meaning that he could no longer have jurisdiction over her. Eventually, it was he who divorced her and her freedom was secured by Emily and Thomas. Joseph was incensed and disinherited both of them and for many years Thomas and his father were estranged. Because Mrs Beecham was awarded alimony, she was able to help Thomas financially, when he was struggling to set up innovative and independent orchestras, especially when his chosen programmes were so esoteric that they only attracted extremely small audiences, consistently losing money. Eventually, after a decade, Joseph Beecham came to appreciate his son's brilliance and began to plough hundreds of thousands of pounds into Thomas's enterprises, thus contributing to the artistic heritage of Britain.

On one of his trips to America, Thomas met and fell in love with Utica Welles. They married in 1903 and had two sons, Adrian, later a composer in his own right and then young Thomas. In 1916, at the age of thirty-seven, Beecham was knighted. His father, by now a Baron, died later the same year, meaning that Sir Thomas inherited the title of Baron as well. Emily never regained her father's love and was the only one of the eight siblings to receive nothing in his will.

Thomas 'discovered' the music of the Bradford-born composer Frederick Delius and included his works in many of his concerts. The two became personal friends and life-long colleagues. Both were frequent visitors to Liverpool, Delius being particularly fond of watching the ships on the River Mersey. Beecham's other favourites were Sibelius, Handel and, above all, Mozart. Such was his admiration for the eighteenth-century genius that, at Beecham's seventieth birthday celebrations, after all the greetings from the glitterati of the musical world had been read out, Beecham asked, 'What? Nothing from Mozart?' He also liked Haydn's compositions but preferred not to employ the harpsichord, claiming that the instrument 'Sounds like two skeletons copulating on a corrugated roof!' On another occasion he described the sound as, 'A birdcage played with a toasting fork!'

Beecham founded or enlarged several notable orchestras, including the Beecham Symphony Orchestra, the Royal Philharmonic, the New Symphony Orchestra and, in collaboration with Sir Malcolm Sargent, the London Philharmonic. Audiences and players alike were astounded by Beecham's capacity for conducting without the need of any score in front of him. Preferring young dynamic musicians, he often signed up promising students or instrumentalists he had chanced upon in theatrical operettas, chamber music ensembles and even in hotel palm-court quartets. Away from the concert halls, he encouraged and joined in with their youthful high spirits. At Crewe railway station, their favourite prank was throwing explosive fireworks onto the platform and rails. At the Adelphi Hotel, Liverpool, Beecham himself unscrewed the bulbs from wall-lights, carried them upstairs in a small table cloth and flung them, one by one, down over the banister to shatter on the marble floor below. He invented his own version of 'Trick or Treat', getting up early, again at the Adelphi, and changing around all the shoes left outside bedroom doors ready to be cleaned and returned.

Realising that audiences might become weary if concert programmes were too heavy or abstruse, Beecham was careful to offer 'Lollipops' to his listeners. These consisted of bright, tuneful and popular pieces, a reward to send his fans home in joyful spirits and encourage them to book tickets again soon.

Engagements in Europe and America frequently kept Beecham away from home and he and Utica drifted apart. Sir Thomas made no secret that he had an eye for the ladies, stating that, 'The trouble with women in an orchestra is that if they're attractive it will upset the players and if they're not it will upset me.'

For over thirty years, Lady Maud Alice Cunard was Beecham's constant companion, mistress and dedicated financial aide. At the same time, among his devoted admirers were Dora Labbette, alias Lisa Perli, who gave birth to Beecham's son, Paul Strang, in 1933, then Mary Dodge, Katherine Heyman and Maud Foster. In 1943, Beecham at last divorced Utica, uncharitably jettisoned Lady Cunard and married Betty Humby, a concert pianist, twenty-nine years his junior. She died in 1958. In less than a year, he married his secretary, Shirley Hudson. He continued to tour and to record with great fervor until his death from thrombosis, two years later.

Of one soprano who screeched her way through a Wagnerian opera, 'Tommy' complained that, 'She sounds like a cart hurtling downhill with the brake full on!' On hearing that Sir Malcolm Sargent had been kidnapped and held prisoner in China, 'Tommy' remarked, 'I'd no idea the Chinese were so musical!'

Dr Anne Biezanek

1927–2010

Rebel with a cause

Raised as a Quaker, Anne converted to the Roman Catholic faith upon her marriage and became devoted to the teachings of her husband's church, attending Mass, Communion and Confession with unfailing fidelity. While deeply in love and happy in her marriage, Anne was still keen to continue with her medical vocation. She was employed as a physician in a mental hospital in Rainhill, Merseyside. In 1961, in her early thirties, she still retained her natural good looks, wide smile and expressive eyes. She was described at that time as, 'tall, handsome, blonde, keenly cerebral, intense and whip-tongued.' Later in her marriage, after five pregnancies, one of which ended in a miscarriage, Anne began to feel the strain of her parenthood/career woman lifestyle.

She loved her husband, her children and her job with equal fervour but the strain of trying to maintain all three began to cause her concern for her own emotional and physical stability. Sensing that unlimited pregnancies were not the blessing to human females that the church alleged, she decided to seek advice from the hospital's Catholic chaplain. When he insisted that she must adhere to the dictates of the religion, she began to question the dogma she had been obeying. She felt trapped in a situation that defied her intellectual logic. The chaplain was adamant, so she decided to ask for a second opinion. Another priest repeated the same edicts. Anne continued in dutiful compliance to be a good wife and a good churchgoer. Within a year, she had a fifth child, followed by a second miscarriage. With the growing demands of home and children, she felt compelled to resign from her post at the hospital. This caused such a drop in the family income that she and her husband could no longer afford their mortgage. They had no alternative but to move in with Anne's parents, who welcomed the young family but found the situation bewildering and disconcerting. In less than six months Anne was pregnant again. After the sixth birth, Anne admitted herself into a mental hospital. She spent five weeks in therapy, returned home and immediately became pregnant again. Anne's parents were so concerned for their daughter's welfare they began to voice their disapproval of the cause of so much distress. Anne had no alternative but to leave her parental home and put her children into foster homes. After a while, loans and charitable funds enabled the Biezaneks and their ever-growing family to move into a smaller house.

But marital relations suffered badly. Anne wrote, 'My husband had to be banished from my presence, into a room of his own. Everything in me that attracted him had to be suppressed. All this I attempted, as Heaven is my witness. Hate became the order of the day. In such an atmosphere even prayer becomes the most dangerous activity. When you pray you must let your defences down. You must lay yourself open to the influence of a loving and generous Spirit. The next thing would be that you find yourself betrayed into kissing your husband good-night.'

To her parents' relief and delight, Anne decided to 'go on the pill'. Her husband advised her to keep her struggles with her faith secret. Instead, she went to her parish priest and confessed that she was practising contraception. He refused to take her confession or give her communion, so she wrote to the pastor of her children's school. His solution was to pretend not to recognise her at communion.

Anne soon felt that she had a financial and medical responsibility to return to work. In her new position, she found herself treating young mothers with already large families, who had had to resort to illegal abortions. The subsequent physical and psychiatric damage was 'terrible'. She felt that these women were no better than slaves or baby machines, her sympathy and empathy arising from her own dilemmas. By the time she was thirty-four she had conceived eleven times, resulting in seven surviving children. Now living in Kinglake Road, Egremont, Wirral, she dared to think the unthinkable. She put these thoughts into practice. Using her own home as the venue, she opened a birth control clinic for married Catholic women. It was the first of its kind anywhere in the world and very soon the press and other media began to ask for interviews. Anne was banned from receiving communion in her own parish, so she took her cause to Westminster Cathedral, requesting assistance from the Archbishop himself. He agreed to give her communion and Anne alerted all the media; enormous publicity ensued.

The embarrassment of all this attention, added to the loss of his conjugal rights, was too much for Anne's husband. An inevitable rift occurred and he left her. Anne saw no point in continuing to follow the Catholic faith and she wrote a book setting forth her medical opinions and the circumstances that had caused her disillusionment. She retrained as a homeopathic doctor and continued to work for the health of others.

Later, when living in Penketh Road, Wallasey, her contention that she had a medical right, as a qualified physician, to prescribe cannabis, brought more adverse publicity. She was charged with 'Possession and Supply'. The press soon picked up on the accusation that she bought cannabis from street traders. The jury acquitted her when she proved that she was prescribing it for her own daughter's medical complaint.

At Dr Anne Biezanek's funeral in 2010, her granddaughter paid tribute to the eighty-three-year-old rebel, saying, 'To me, she was my Gran, but she was also a fiery person who had strong opinions. She changed the world for Catholic women who were forbidden to use birth control. She gave them the courage to demand it.'

Lord Birkenhead (F.E. Smith)
1872–1930

Frederick Edwin Smith – 'Better Informed!'

'Before the war there were hardly any taxes yet we spent half our lives complaining about those!' No, not a quote from Ken Dodd, but from a predecessor by at least a hundred years – and the war in question was the First World War. F.E. Smith, the 1st Earl of Birkenhead, had a love/hate relationship with money, bringing repercussions which lasted even beyond his death.

Born in Birkenhead, Wirral, and christened Frederick, the same name as his father, the head of a flourishing property firm, young Freddie was always known as F.E. in order to avoid confusion.

In later years, when F.E. had achieved much acclaim and many honours, as well as a notorious reputation for wild living, an old lady in Birkenhead asked her friend, 'Effie Smith? Effie Smith? Who's she then?' To which the other granny replied, 'I don't know but I don't think she can be a modest girl, to be talked about so much!'

F.E. would certainly have appreciated the humour of this situation, being himself a man of great wit with infamous predilections for alcohol, fast horses and disreputable behaviour. In his more sober moments, he was also a brilliant orator with an incisive brain and a huge capacity for any legal or political agenda.

As an infant he attended a small private school in the Wirral, run single-handedly by Mrs Kate Lewis. Unfortunately, this early example of female wisdom and organisational skills did nothing to influence his opinion of female intelligence nor professional suitability. He remained a lifelong opponent of distaff admission to the Bar, politics or to any other profession. A preparatory school in Southport guided his next steps in education. As this was before the construction of the Mersey Tunnel, the Liverpool ferries served as part of his regular journeys.

Failing the entrance to Harrow was a blow to his already high self-esteem and Birkenhead School was the alternative. After that came two years at Liverpool University and from there he became an undergraduate at Wadham College, Oxford. Grasping the opportunity to have a wild time, F.E. indulged his irresponsible streak by running up enormous debts for tailoring, sports equipment, alcohol and books. All the while, however, he was gaining esteem as a scintillating and entertaining adversary in university debates. Showing that he could knuckle down when necessary, he revised stoically and graduated with a First in law, followed by three years as a Fellow of Merton College.

For recreation, this daredevil exhibitionist loved horse riding, caring little for his frequent falls nor for the private lands over which he trespassed. This man of law cheerfully ignored minor bye-laws when it suited him. However, for all his high living he couldn't abide snobbery, often boasting of his own lowly start in life. But poverty is relative – his father was a solid middle-class businessman whose income was secure enough for him to leave his firm as a mature student in order to study law. F.E.'s own natural charm and burgeoning career brought him many social invitations from upper-crust hostesses. At one event, a lady introduced herself as 'Mrs Porter-Porter, with a hyphen.' Thinking immediately only of the dark ale of the same name, F.E. replied, 'And I'm Whisky-Whisky with a siphon!'

A career in law demands infinite dedication to detail, great perspicacity, eloquence and self-belief. F.E. was a supreme example of these qualities. From the earliest days of his vocation he was considered to be a powerful advocate, initially in Liverpool and then in London. His off-the-cuff responses have become legend. One tetchy judge complained, 'I have listened at length to your speech but I am still no wiser.'

'No wiser, my Lord but far better informed,' was F.E.'s cheeky reply. On another occasion he was accused by a judge of being personally offensive. The response was, 'As a matter of fact we *both* are. The difference is that I am trying to be. But you just can't help it.'

His quick thinking was more often used for better purposes. Defending on behalf of an insurance company against a youth who claimed industrial injury at work, F.E. sympathetically asked the claimant to 'show the court how little you can raise your arm now. Thank you. And show how high you could raise it before the accident.' The stupid boy duly obliged.

Among his many influential clients, he was a favourite of Lord Leverhulme of Port Sunlight, the soap magnate whose favourite hobby seemed to be litigation against all and sundry, especially his suppliers of raw materials. Successful though their association was, the two men could not have been more different, Leverhulme being of extremely Spartan and totally abstemious principles (see *Liverpool's Own*).

In 1901, F.E. married Margaret Eleanor Furneaux, settling in to no. 2 Cavendish Road on the edge of Birkenhead Park. They later had two daughters and a son. Subsequently they moved to The Grove, Thornton Hough, Wirral. Despite his disdainful opinion of female suitability for professional life, he always deferred to Margaret's opinion in matters domestic, legal and even political.

Licensing work in Liverpool brought excellent fees, especially in September and October, the season of Annual Licensing Sessions. Unlike others, in his early days F.E. was not at all conscientious with the preparation of cases, relying on his juniors or his own ready wit. He once turned up at court, was handed a brief on arrival, had no time to study this, but spoke to the solicitor, saying, 'My friend and colleague has given me the greatest of assistance in this case, for which I am greatly indebted. Now tell me, what is your opinion in this matter?' The solicitor was flattered by being consulted so charmingly and answered in great detail, enabling F.E. to proceed with a superlative presentation of the defence, with added compliments to the 'learned and knowledgeable' solicitor. The client was delighted with the successful result and treated them all to a celebratory lunch at the Adelphi. In 1908, F.E. was made a King's Counsel. One of his more notorious cases was the defence of Ethel le Neve, the girlfriend of Dr Crippen. Thanks to Smith, she was acquitted of the murder of Crippen's wife. In a separate trial, Crippen was convicted.

Among Smith's admirable deeds was the fact that he volunteered for service in the First World War, providing the *Liverpool Post* and *Echo* with the tongue-in-cheek headline, 'ENGLAND SAFE! F.E. JOINS THE TERRITORIALS!' In order to become head of the Government's Press Bureau, he was promoted to colonel. In 1915 he served in France as a major with the Indian Corps.

Smith's dazzling performances in court had made him an ideal candidate for membership of the government. In 1918, he became the Conservative Member of Parliament for West Derby, Liverpool, which also incorporated, at that time, much of Walton. This brought him into direct contact with Lloyd George and Churchill. 'Networking' was natural to F.E. and he set about cultivating acquaintances with all the 'right' people. Lloyd George offered him the post of Speaker of the House of Commons. F.E. wanted to consult his wife but Margaret was away at the time, so he allowed Churchill to persuade him to accept. Following this he became Lord Chancellor – now, the man who couldn't control his own finances took charge of the National Purse! His success can be measured by the knighthood conferred in 1919. That same year, at only forty-seven, Sir F.E. Smith was created Baron Birkenhead, thereby entitling him to enter the House of Lords. Now a peer of the realm, as with his other appointments, Lord Birkenhead excelled at his post and was a model of propriety and rectitude at all times, contributing greatly to the progress of the nation. In 1924, he was appointed Secretary of State for India. In this post, his sensitive understanding of the social and religious divisions between Muslims and Hindus was greatly helped by his earlier experiences in Liverpool during the disputes between Catholics and Protestants. In 1926, his behind-the-scenes efforts to avoid or at least minimise the General Strike were acknowledged and praised even by his opponents in the Labour Party.

Privately, however, he was still unable to curb his own extravagances. With prosperity came further excesses; extensions to his house, with stables for more horses than he could possible ride, alcohol, lavish hospitality. Some of this was due to the mistaken belief that he would inherit a fortune from his friend and client, Houston, the shipping magnate. But Houston's young second wife put paid to previous promises, eventually sharing the millions with Houston's secretary. F.E. had already spent the 'phantom' inheritance and apart from his £5,000 pension and a few directorships, he was left destitute.

His life was cut short at the age of fifty-eight by an attack of pneumonia. He had been in poor health for two years, and was taken ill on holiday in Biarritz, France, the favourite playground of the rich and famous. His home and investments were worth £63,000 but, after payments to creditors, his wife, Margaret, was left penniless, dependent upon charity from Lord Beaverbook and other stalwart friends. Thus, his children were able to continue their education and Margaret was assured of a respectable existence until her death in 1968.

Maud Carpenter OBE
1895–1977

Doyenne of the Liverpool Playhouse Theatre

A sturdy sixteen-year-old, who had temporarily worked with her older sister in the box office at the now-defunct Kelly's Theatre in Paradise Street, transferred, in 1911, to the box office at the Liverpool Playhouse Theatre in Williamson Square. Young Maud Carpenter worked diligently, displaying a natural flair for accountancy and an inherent skill for organisation. Even more importantly, she quickly developed a fierce loyalty to the theatre itself. She settled in and thus began a lifetime's devotion to the welfare and excellent reputation of the Playhouse.

Such was her dedication that, by 1922, Maud had worked her way up to the post of Administrator. Her commitment to the overall success of this nationally respected repertory company ensured its survival throughout many financial ups and downs, the dangers of two world wars and the prospective rivalry of the early days of television.

Maud's unswerving support was equally as important as that of the solid pillars in the auditorium. Often referred to as the Unofficial Mayoress of Liverpool, Maud remained the driving force of the theatre until her retirement in 1962. In total, she had worked at the Playhouse for fifty-one years.

In her mature years, Maud's imposing stature and precisely conventional approach to the fashions of her day, gave her an aura that impressed audiences, boards of governors, actors and artistic directors, all of whom regarded her with respect and affection. During her tenure and even later, the stage and the baroque Victorian-style auditorium were graced by many aspiring thespians who subsequently became much-loved celebrities. Richard Briers has very happy memories, as it was here that he met his wife, Ann Davies. The courtship of Sir Michael Redgrave and Rachel Kempson also took place backstage in Liverpool, as did the romance of Rex Harrison and the second of his six wives, Lili Palmer. David Suchet and Sheila Ferris also tied the knot while associated with the Playhouse and there are those who claim to have seen Trevor Eve and Sharon Maughan there together in their courting days.

From the point of view of audiences, the Playhouse became a focal point of theatrical outings. Many middle-class matrons bought season tickets and their 'three weekly' visits to each new production, provided opportunities to meet friends, enjoy the varied choice of plays and partake of the excellent coffee and biscuits on sale during the intervals. The sweet aroma of coffee permeating the stalls and circle always created the best possible greeting, even before the two piano duets and overture began. Maud, herself, was often on hand to grace the proceedings and to greet regulars. Maud felt that audiences appreciated good taste in the choice of plays, scenery and costume. Frequently, the stylish set designs would elicit their own round of applause as soon as the curtain rose.

Maud had no ambitions to appear on stage, but she was quite a character in her own right, in fact, an amalgam of two characters; the redoubtable Hyacinth Bucket, as played by Birkenhead's own Patricia Routledge and the risible Mrs Malaprop in Sheridan's *School For Scandal*. This was because Maud's elegant appearance belied her lack of further education and the absence of any middle-class elocution lessons. Maud's confused expressions resulted in some of her well-remembered utterances. For instance, she boasted that she had sailed around the Venetian canal system in a Lagonda, she also claimed that she couldn't go into any of the newly decorated backstage dressing rooms because she was 'lethargic to paint' and she thought that Ibsen's *The Wild Duck* was another of 'them Gawd-awful bird plays.'

But her heart was certainly in the right place. She was a very 'hands-on' administrator, often helping to borrow suitable items of furniture or costume for productions – even highly valuable jewels for pre-publicity photographs for one play. These, however, were then returned to the jeweller and skillfully re-created for the rest of the run by using fruit-jelly sweets. Maud wanted her actors and actresses to be regarded as equally glamorous as any Hollywood starlets, insisting that they must dress elegantly on all occasions, even off duty. The jeans and trainers of today's actors would have been unheard of in her day. She once reprimanded a young Anthony Hopkins for his casual style of dress. She also refused to allow her cast to arrive at the stage-door on foot. They were expected to roll up in taxis, at the very least. Once, when a new rain-soaked and bedraggled young actor arrived in her office, she immediately jumped to the conclusion that he must be a workman. She tried to dismiss him with a wave of her hand, saying that all her backstage staff were on long-term contracts.

'Go to the Royal Court, up the road,' she commanded. 'They take on temps as and when needed.'

Through the years, many directors, then known as producers, became Maud's colleagues. As ever in artistic circles, their personalities and approaches to the enterprise were varied. Maud adapted and worked diligently with each one. She had a determined nature and made sure that the progress of the theatre went from strength to strength. During the Second World War, Maud volunteered for night-time fire-watching on the roof of the theatre, situated as it is in the very heart of the city. Maud's personal method of protection from the infamous May Blitz was to shake her fists at the enemy planes and to shout out to the pilots, demanding that they must avoid bombing her beloved theatre. Even they obeyed her!

After she had been awarded both the OBE and an Honorary Degree from Liverpool University, Maud became even more aware of her own position in society, boasting that she now lived 'on the Wirral,' a prestigious address, considered superior to Liverpool.

'I have a beautiful house,' she said, preening herself like a pedigree cat. 'It's truly wonderful, I've got everything a millionaire could wish for, only on a smaller scale.' Such airs and graces certainly impressed her young company. One day, Maud had to make an emergency flying visit to London to obtain the necessary license then legally required for the next production, from the Lord Chamberlain, Nelson King. This was due to an oversight on the part of the producer. But the play could not possibly go on without legal permission. Maud had to wait in London while King read and passed the play. She then sent a terse telegram, the equivalent to today's texts, saying, 'Seen King. All well. Maud.' Thinking she'd met King George, several actors and stagehands rushed to Lime Street station to greet Maud on her return. Some were bearing bouquets for her. Presumably hyacinths.

Kim Cattrall

Sex and the City of Liverpool

How to describe Kim Cattrall? Her millions of television and cinema fans would no doubt say 'sexy', 'sassy' and 'classy', but there is more to Kim Cattrall than just Samantha Jones. Her theatre aficionados would add 'classical', 'enterprising' and 'versatile'. The Hollywood and television star was already an experienced and highly regarded 'legitimate' actress long before she became one of the flirtatious four career girls who swished their way around the hot spots of New York.

Born in Mossley Hill, Liverpool, Kim was only three months old when her parents, Denis and Shane (née Baugh) Cattrall, emigrated to Canada. Kim was brought up in Courtenay, British Columbia, until the age of eleven. She returned to Liverpool when her grandmother was taken ill. Kim stayed with her great aunt Mai in Wavertree and became a pupil at St Edmund's College for Girls, Princes Park. In her spare time, Kim took the London Academy of Music and Dramatic Art examinations. This entailed preparing two or three contrasting audition speeches and performing them on stage in the empty auditorium of the Crane/Neptune (now Brian Epstein) theatre, in Hanover Street, Liverpool. An external examiner would sit alone in the darkened stalls to assess the candidate and grade the results. Kim's marks were always high, maybe partly because her aunts took her to see various plays and musical productions at the Liverpool Playhouse and the Royal Court Theatre. They frequently visited family relatives in several parts of Merseyside. Kim still has aunts, cousins and second cousins in Widnes, Wirral, Aigburth and Burscough. During her early teens Kim was unaware of the drama concerning her own family saga. In 2009, with the help of BBC researchers on the *Who Do You Think You Are?* programme, Kim discovered that her grandfather, George Baugh, had disappeared in 1938, deserting his wife and three daughters, one of them being Kim's mother, Shane, who was aged eight at the time. The Baugh family were left penniless in Toxteth and they never saw him again. A great deal of detective work at the BBC eventually revealed that George had met another woman, Isabella Oliver in Tudhoe, County Durham. He bigamously married her while still legally married to Kim's grandmother. Kim was able to trace records showing that he then had a further family of four children and that they all emigrated to Australia in 1961. After making contact with these half brothers and sisters via the programme, Kim's aunts actually met some of them and established a connection that would have been impossible without the revelations discovered in the series.

Kim, herself, left Liverpool at the age of sixteen. When her father came to take her back to Canada, she was most reluctant to leave the area where she had family and friends. She completed her final years at high school in Canada and then went to New York to enrol at the American Academy of Dramatic Arts. Upon graduation, Otto Preminger offered her a five-year contract and she starred in his 1975 movie *Rosebud*. In 1976, however, Universal Studios bought out that contract and proceeded to book her into numerous leading guest roles in episodes of *Columbo*, *Quincy* and *The Incredible Hulk*. While working on the *Star Trek* VII series, she decided to invest in a little personal publicity. She persuaded a photographer to come to the studio and, using the backdrop of the Enterprise Bridge

scenery, he shot pictures of her entirely nude except for her Vulcan ears. When a furious Leonard Nimoy discovered this, he had the negatives destroyed.

A different bridge became an important part of Kim's career when she starred in Arthur Miller's stage play *A View from the Bridge*. Chekhov's *Three Sisters* was another theatrical production which won critical acclaim for the now classical actress. But Kim's physical charms were again in demand for her 'Pepsi One' commercials, as well as for Tetley Tea and for Nissan. So steamy were they that they were withdrawn by New Zealand television stations. However, Kim and her third husband successfully collaborated in writing a best-selling book entitled *Satisfaction: The Art of the Female Orgasm*.

In total, Kim has had three husbands and a long-standing partnership. Her marriage to Larry Davis from 1977 to 1979, was annulled. While married to Andre Lyson (1982–9), she lived with him in Frankfurt and learned to converse in German. Mark Levinson, her spouse from 1998 to 2004, was an audio designer as well as a writer while her recent partnership with restaurateur Alan Wyse, twenty years her junior, ended in 2009.

In December 1988, a woman's prerogative to change her mind saved Kim's life. She was booked on the Pan Am 103 flight from London to New York but cancelled at the last moment to do some more Christmas shopping. This was the plane that ended in tragic disaster over Lockerbie.

Kim's film titles include *Police Academy*, *Big Trouble in Little China*, *Mannequin* and *Porky's*. Then came the phenomenon of the several series and two cinema films of *Sex and the City*. Tens of millions of viewers gave worldwide adulation and acclaim and so famous did Kim become, as her alter-ego the man-eating Samantha Jones, that the public began to forget her other achievements. However, her next appearance on British television was as the drab and dowdy wife of Rudyard Kipling in the true story of the writer's search for his son, lost in battle during the First World War. But once again, her now fifty-two year-old naked beauty was displayed, when the BBC commissioned Tom Hunter to re-create a twenty-first century version of Titian's *Diana and Actaeon*, in a form suitable for sales abroad. This was in order to secure enough funds for Britain to keep the $50,000,000 work of art on public display in the UK.

In 2008, the theatre world of London's West End was fortunate enough to engage Ms Cattrall to star in Brian Clark's play *Whose Life is it Anyway?* He had adapted the script from his own 1972 television play. It was originally written as a vehicle for a male star and the plot concerns a sculptor, paralysed from the neck down after a car accident. The sculptor sees no point in a life without art. He wishes to die but doctors and psychiatrists refuse his request for euthanasia. Such a theme might be seen as depressing and disturbing but it is written with a great deal of black humour and a fair share of suggestive innuendo. Tom Conti was a great success in an earlier production but in the latest adaptation the main protagonist is a sculptress, and starred the multi-talented Kim Cattrall. For someone who had risen to international fame displaying her feminine pulchritude, lying as though turned to marble herself, and acting with only her voice and facial expressions was a tremendous challenge. Kim's ability to communicate emotion and bleak humour gained her new fans among the many who had never heard of *Sex and the City*.

The following year, Kim again wowed West End audiences, this time with her interpretation of Noel Coward's Amanda in *Private Lives*. Her 'cut glass' upper-class accent of the 1930s era was a delight. Her partner in this stylish love-hate relationship was Matthew MacFadyen and they were a well-balanced, convincing duo, despite the fact that in reality he was over twenty years her junior. Kim reprised the role in Toronto and in 2011 took the show to Broadway. Between the two *Private Lives* appearances, the Liverpool Playhouse, under the artistic direction of Gemma Bodinez, managed to persuade Ms Cattrall to star in their production of Shakespeare's *Antony and Cleopatra*. The negotiations had taken two years to complete due to Ms Cattrall's busy schedule. This time, Kim's character, Cleopatra, the Egyptian Diva, was the younger of the two lovers. Mark Antony, in Shakespeare's interpretation, is an ageing figure and Jeffery Kissoon played the role. Together the two ensured box-office sell-outs for the whole run and enthusiastic audiences gave standing ovations at every performance. The girl born on the banks of the Mersey triumphed as the Queen of the Nile.

While in Liverpool, Kim made it clear in all interviews how much she enjoyed returning to Merseyside, rekindling childhood memories and being with her extended family. At the conclusion of her five-week triumph she bade a fond farewell, saying, 'I come from a long line of Scouse women. When I came back to Merseyside and saw the skyline, my heart soared. Hopefully I will be back soon. I had such a lovely time here.'

Edward & Margaret Chambré Hardman

1889–1988 & 1909–70

Monday morning:

'What shall we have for breakfast, this morning, my dear? Shall we have boiled eggs?'

'Yes, that would be very nice. And a cup of tea.'

'I'll just take some clean egg cups and tea cups out of the cupboard and boil a kettle of water on the gas ring.'

Monday afternoon:

'What shall we have for tea, my dear? Shall we have a couple of boiled eggs?'

'Yes, that would be very nice. And perhaps some toast with Golden Syrup spread on it. And a cup of tea. But our cups and egg cups are still dirty from this morning.'

'Yes. We've been so busy in the studio and the darkroom, I haven't had a moment to wash up. Never mind, I'll just take some more clean crockery out of the cupboard.'

Tuesday morning:

Wednesday morning:

Thursday morning:

Friday morning:

'What shall we have for breakfast, my dear? Shall we have boiled eggs and a cup of tea?'

'I'll just take some clean crockery out of the cupboard. I haven't had time to wash up all week.'

Dear Reader, you can guess the rest! In their professional capacity as society photographers to the gentry of Merseyside, Chester and North Wales, Mr and Mrs Chambré Hardman were meticulously efficient and well-organised but, once the door between the business area in no. 59 Rodney Street, Liverpool, and their private apartment closed, clutter, confusion and eccentricity reigned supreme.

Dishes were never washed, simply put aside and forgotten about. Dozens of clean egg cups were stored in readiness for the next frugal meal. Unused tablets of perfumed soap filled every drawer in their small bedroom with its direct view of the Anglican cathedral (built during Edward's lifetime). Bundles of elegant lingerie and clothing spilled out of the single wardrobe, to fill the numerous heavy leather suitcases, which doubled as permanent extra storage, in the bedroom and sitting room. On top of the wardrobe there is still a box full of dry bones destined for, but never eaten by, their dog. Two huge, circular tables made from Burmese copper rice steamers, a genuine Lalique table lamp, two bicycles and an ARP sergeant's uniform complete with gas mask, adorned the living quarters. Nothing was ever thrown away. Collections of pebbles and shells from the seaside and a bath that was never plumbed in still reside in the cellar, next to the underground room where their female employees worked in the makeshift darkroom. In spite of all this, the business ran smoothly and was highly successful, earning an excellent reputation as the most desirable place for debutantes, high-ranking military and naval officers and well-to-do family

groups to sit for elegant and flattering photographic portraits. Ladies would often arrive with hatboxes and suitcases full of alternative ensembles before eventually deciding on their favourite outfit. An elegant and very private changing room with a huge mirror was provided for this purpose. This room, and several others, also had a wash basin. These dated from previous occupancies by the many specialist doctors who had their consulting rooms in Rodney Street.

The lady receptionist who dealt with all telephone enquiries was carefully tutored to make the 'correct' suggestions as to the size, quality and design of frame for each portrait. There was the 'Gold' standard or the 'Standard' standard, according to price. Naturally, most patrons felt obliged to opt for the gold standard. The result was a Bentley car and a very large gramophone for the Hardmans and chocolate éclairs for the staff. Margot Fonteyn, Ivor Novello, Robert Donat and a very young Patricia Routledge were but a few of the many theatrical celebrities who flocked to either the Bold Street, Rodney Street or Chester studios in order to pay their three guinea fees for publicity images. These were always skillfully retouched to airbrush out even the tiniest blemishes or crow's feet. The results are still on display in 59 Rodney Street, now owned and lovingly maintained by

Dr Geoff Woodcock photographed on his fourth birthday by Edward Chambré Hardman.

the National Trust, supported by the Heritage Trust. Every item is authentically original and carefully preserved, creating a 'living' museum and testament to this fascinating bygone age.

A recorded interview given to BBC Radio Merseyside in 1975 allows visitors to hear Edward's own voice, with his pleasantly modulated, upper middle-class pronunciation, bearing no hint of any regional accent. Margaret's birth certificate shows Rainhill, Merseyside, as the register office, but indicating that Rainhill was, at that time, designated as being part of West Derby East. Margaret was a highly intelligent, artistic and outgoing girl, fond of various sports and with an obvious aptitude for management and clerical skills. She attended the prestigious Blackburn House School for Girls, situated on Hope Street between the Philharmonic Hall and the Anglican cathedral, facing the College of Art.

As a young man, Edward was self-taught and considered himself to be an artist. When he decided he needed a capable and willing assistant, he approached the headmistress of Blackburn House, enquiring if there were any suitable candidates among her pupils. Margaret Hills was suggested and proved herself to be more than perfect in both enthusiasm for the subject and competence in dealing with staff and with discerning clientele. Edward quickly increased her managerial responsibilities and soon realised how much he cared for her on a personal level. Due to the age gap, however, he was reticent in declaring his feelings. Margaret returned his affection and, being a lively young woman in the Flapper mould, became impatient with this procrastination. Taking herself off to Paisley in Scotland, she found a position there for several months. Dozens of love letters, however, travelled between them. Eventually, Margaret returned and the two sealed their union. A wedding photograph shows Margaret in a dark blue lace dress. It is still on display at the Rodney Street house.

The married couple became constant companions, cycling out to rural destinations to capture the landscapes with their expensive cameras. This was their hobby while the upper crust portraits were their bread and butter. An unoccupied bedroom was artistically designed by Margaret to suit any age of client. Greek columns provided a classical frame for almost any adult, a rocking swan easily accommodated toddlers, while an imitation leopard skin rug made an equally stylish resting place for babies or coquettish young women.

Frank Cottrell Boyce

Ambassador for the pleasure of reading

'I really believe that an ability to enjoy books is one of the greatest gifts we can give our children. Everyone loves to be read to.'

Frank Cottrell Boyce

Frank certainly practices what he preaches. Over the past few years he has pursued a personal campaign to bring the love of literature to as wide an audience as possible. Many schools and libraries in Merseyside and ever further afield have played host to his entertaining and thought-provoking literary celebrations. Using his own award-winning books as appetisers, Frank opens the proceedings with a lively reading then engages the youngsters in conversations and question-and-answer sessions. Unlike most classroom situations, it is the pupils who ask the questions and Frank who supplies the answers. Although he always relishes this, unexpected predicaments can sometimes occur.

'I once did a reading to a group of very large, very disaffected boys in Glasgow,' he recalls:

When I got to a particularly exciting cliff-hanger, I stopped and asked for questions. It went like this. First, a big strong boy, put up his hand, 'What happens next?'
Me: 'Well I'm pleased you want to know. Why not get the book out of the library and read on? Next question?'
Second, even bigger boy: 'Can you read us a bit more?'
Me: 'Well I'm here to encourage you to read. So do get the book out of the library and read the next bit . . . from page fifty-seven. That's where I stopped.'
Third boy, so massive, the weather changed when he put up his hand – and the earth quivered when he spoke: 'WOULD YE *just* READ, wee man?!!'
Me: 'OK!'

One thing Frank doesn't like to see in modern schools is those areas that once were the library corners but are now sacrificed to Learning Resource Centres, with valuable, long-life books chucked out and rapidly-dating computers installed instead. He quotes his own daughter's words of wisdom when she comments, 'Every single school kid, these days, has access to a computer at home. Hardly any of the children in my school has any meaningful literature at home.'

Frank's own school days were spent in various parts of Merseyside, including St Alphonsus' in Kirkdale, St Bartholomew's in Rainhill, and De La Salle in St Helens. He recalls one very special teacher in particular, with whom he not only studied Shakespeare and all the classical authors but also did a very successful Punch and Judy show for a couple of years. A doctorate in English Literature at Oxford University completed his education. For the last twelve years he and his wife and family have lived in Crosby.

Film and television scripts were some of Frank's early successes. The BAFTA- and Oscar-nominated feature film, *Hilary and Jackie*, concerning the life of concert cellist Jacqueline Du Pré, was shot entirely in Liverpool, with the elegant interiors of the Three Graces Buildings doubling for scenes supposedly filmed in Moscow. Another film, *Welcome to Sarajevo*, was given a special screening inside the White House, Washington DC, at the personal request of the then president, Bill Clinton.

Writing for *Coronation Street*, *Emmerdale* and later many episodes of *Brookside* and its spin-off, *Damon and Debbie*, proved invaluable experience in the creating of naturally flowing dialogue and strong characterisations. In the twenty-first century, Frank began writing fiction with a wide appeal for children and teenagers. From the outset, their success was phenomenal. His very first novel, *Millions*, won the Carnegie Medal. His book *Cosmic* received more five-star reviews than any other children's story in the USA and was short-listed for the Carnegie Medal. *Framed* was short-listed for both the Whitbread Book of the Year and the Carnegie Medal while his stage play, *Proper Clever* was produced at the Liverpool Playhouse, as part of the European Capital of Culture Year 2008. In 2009, Frank adapted *Framed* as the screenplay for a BBC television programme. In 2011, Frank's book, *The Unforgotten Coat*, was his gift to the Reader Organisation's 'Our Read' project. He was delighted that 50,000 copies were given away in supermarkets, libraries, coffee bars, train and bus stations and the Beatles Museum, Albert Dock, as an encouragement to reluctant readers who never buy books nor visit a library.

As well as being very active in the Reader Organisation, in association with its director, Dr Jane Davis, Frank is a patron of the Liverpool educational charity, the John Moores Trust.

In addition to his own creations, Frank is breathing new life into the work of another world-famous author, Ian Fleming, the celebrated writer of the James Bond phenomenon, who also wrote the children's favourite *Chitty Chitty Bang Bang* – so popular was this book that is was adapted by Roald Dahl for the 1968 film and, later, the musical version toured as a spectacular theatrical show. In 2010, the Fleming family invited Frank Cottrell Boyce to imagine what might happen in a more up-to-date metamorphosis. So Chitty takes flight again, in the twenty-first century, initially as a VW campervan, eventually reverting to its original manifestation.

In 2011, as well as working on a new project with Colin Firth, Frank was one of the welcoming committee for Dolly Parton when she met Lord Mayor of Liverpool, Frank Prendergast, at the launch of the new Reading Village and Imagination Library in Everton. Dolly's own charitable organisation sends a book per month to new-born children until they are five, to encourage a love of reading.

Like the ripples of a stone thrown into a lake, Frank's enterprises spread ever wider. One of the special moments in his life came when he acted as compère during the Papal Vigil in London's Hyde Park. The opening ceremony of the 2012 London Olympic Games also owes its inception to Frank's imaginative creativity. Working with the Oscar-winning director of *Slumdog Millionaire*, Danny Boyle, and with a host of choreographers, musicians and technical experts, the breathtaking spectacle gradually comes to life. The size of the worldwide audience is astounding.

'If a hundred thousand people read one of my books or sees one of my films, that is a great success,' he says. 'A billion people watch the Olympics! It's an amazing thought.'

Sir Samuel Cunard

1787–1865

Merseyside's favourite Canadian

Samuel Cunard was the man who, more successfully than any other, created the 'ocean highway' between the British Isles and North America. In recent years the River Mersey has been thrilled to greet, at various times, the gigantic queens of the sea, the *QE2*, the *Queen Mary 2*, the *Queen Victoria* and the *Queen Elizabeth*, all floating palaces of luxury and leisure. Thousands are delighted to travel on such prestigious liners. Thousands more are pleased to give a royal reception to these majestic vessels as they steam into the Mersey Estuary.

Young Samuel's parents, Abraham Cunard, of German origins and Quaker beliefs, and Margaret née Murphy, from Irish Catholic ancestry, settled in Halifax, Nova Scotia, Canada, from America in 1783. Abraham was a master carpenter and timber merchant. Samuel was a lively, intelligent and ambitious youngster. By the age of seventeen he was already managing his own general store. He later went into partnership with his father, extending their business to include the transport of coal and iron. In 1812, when the

Anglo-American War began, Cunard joined the Second Battalion, the Halifax Regiment and was soon promoted to captain. At the conclusion of his military service he returned to Halifax and took on several high-ranking civic responsibilities including Lighthouse Commissioner. He was known to be an honest and charitable businessman. He married Susan Duffus in 1815, who bore him nine children but who died in 1828, only thirteen years after their wedding.

Cunard became a highly successful businessman and a leading figure in Nova Scotia. When developing his shipping enterprises, he had the foresight to realise that steam would rapidly outclass sail for speed and reliability. By the late 1830s, the Industrial Revolution made it imperative to provide faster transportation of mail and raw materials across the Atlantic. Hearing that the Victorian government was inviting tenders to provide a fleet of steamships, Cunard joined forces with the eminent marine engineer, Robert Napier, and submitted a bid to build four ships, thereby guaranteeing fortnightly Atlantic crossings throughout the year, no matter how bad the weather. He travelled to England to put in his bid personally. In 1839 his contract for a regular mail and cargo service was granted. With the ship owners David McIver of Liverpool and George Burns of Glasgow, he inaugurated the British and North American Royal Mail Steam Packet Company. Their four, wooden paddle-steamers began sailing between Liverpool and Boston in 1840. A change of name to Cunard Steamships Limited soon followed.

Now a widower of many years, Samuel settled permanently in Britain. His steamship *Britannia*'s maiden voyage from Liverpool to Halifax, Nova Scotia, continuing to Boston, Massachusetts, instituted consistent cargo and passenger crossings. Ever considerate of his passengers and crew, Cunard instigated an immutable policy of 'Safety Before Speed'. With uncanny intuition, he forbade all his captains to undertake any action which might place any ship in a hazardous situation. Caution paid dividends in respect of the company's ongoing unblemished history and accident-free reputation.

In 1859, Queen Victoria conferred the title of Baronet upon Cunard in honour of his outstanding contribution to British maritime development. Sir Samuel was not actively religious in private nor public life, being regarded as agnostic rather than an atheist in his views. However, his actions spoke louder than words, being always considerate, tolerant and generous. Human rights were more important to him than rituals and dogma. On hearing that one of his passengers had been discriminated against due to the colour of his skin, Cunard was outraged and stated publicly, 'I can assure you that nothing of this kind will ever again take place on any ship with which I am connected.'

In matters of practicality, Cunard became the proprietor of several Canadian companies. He also owned logging projects and coal companies, providing all the fuel for his fleets. For a time, he owned more than a eighth of Prince Edward Island in the Gulf of St Lawrence, near Halifax.

Sir Samuel's death was in Kensington, London, and he is buried in Brompton Cemetery. He was succeeded by his eldest son, who inherited the title and became Sir Edward Cunard, continuing the ever-prospering business, eventually absorbing other companies including the ill-fated White Star Line.

Since 2006, there has been a memorial statue on the Waterfront at Halifax, Canada. If you wish to see a memorial in Britain, visit the River Mersey when any of the beautiful Cunarders pay a visit, especially in 2015, when the river plays host to a whole dynasty of Queens.

The 13th Earl of Derby and David Ross

Edward Smith Stanley, 1775–1851

Knowsley's 13th Earl of Derby
Knowsley Safari Park

There have been Earls of Derby on Merseyside since 1485, when Thomas Stanley was created the first earl as a reward for his loyalty to Henry Tudor. At that time, Knowsley was part of the administrative domain of West Derby, hence the title 'of Derby'.

Throughout the centuries the 'Stanley' Earls have played immensely important roles in the military, political and social life of England. The 5th Earl was a patron of William Shakespeare, while later owners of the title have provided one Foreign Secretary, one Secretary of State, a President of the Board of Trade, a Governor General of Canada, a Minister of War during the First World War and, in 1780, the inaugurator of the famous 'Derby' Horse Race.

Edward Smith Stanley, the 13th Earl, however, had no aspirations in the field of battle nor the world of politics. Instead, from a very early age, he showed an innate interest in

Edward Smith Stanley, the 13th Earl of Derby.

nature and the animal kingdom. As his parents separated when he was only three years old, he lived with his father, at Knowsley Hall with its 2,000 acres of parkland, until he went to Eton and later Trinity College, Cambridge, where he graduated with an MA in 1795.

In his more mature years, his interest in politics and civic affairs was so minimal that he was glad to hand over such responsibilities as soon as his son, also called Edward, showed an inclination in those directions.

The 13th Earl, Lord Stanley, lived in a era when many, such as Isaac Newton, James Watt and Richard Arkwright, were furthering knowledge and technology, while in other fields biologists like Sweden's Carl Linnaeus were diligently identifying and classifying flora and fauna from all over the world. Lord Stanley's own scientific interest in mammals and ornithology prompted him to embark upon a series of collections of creatures from far and wide. He was a founding member of the Zoological Society and, in 1831, he became its President.

Within the sandstone walls of the Knowsley estate, Lord Stanley designed a protective environment, with sheltering suitable for the specimens he was commissioning from explorers and freelance collectors all around the world. He called this menagerie his Aviary but the residents were by no means only birds. His assistants brought to Britain numerous animals never previously seen outside their native lands. His intention was to catalogue, breed and encourage the spread of endangered or particularly attractive species, such as the many colourful birds which were his own particular favourites. To facilitate this, he created a lake with its own island, as well as planting more tress, widening the pathways to accommodate horse-drawn vehicles and, for the villagers, improving local cottages and building St Mary's Church. He also wanted to provide illustrations of these creatures for a wider public, quite a problem before the invention of the camera.

Among the earl's notable colleagues, the humorous poet Edward Lear proved to be a great friend and a highly esteemed asset. This multi-talented musician, raconteur and writer of the children's poem 'The Owl and the Pussy Cat' was also an immensely gifted artist. The two men first met when Lord Stanley visited Regent's Park in London. Lear was drawing the bird life and another young man, John Thompson, was supervising the welfare of the animals. Lord Stanley brought them both to Knowsley, putting Johnson in charge of thirty zoo keepers and inviting Lear to stay with the family and produce accurate and appealing depictions of the wildlife. Lear's vibrant watercolour of a Golden Parakeet is still on display in Knowsley Hall, as are his delightful studies of zebras, eland antelopes and guanaco llamas. Lear became a great favourite with the children of the Stanley family, spending many happy hours entertaining them with his stories, rhymes and songs. So integrated did he become, it seemed only natural that the words Lear and earl are perfect anagrams.

In spite of a partial paralysis, following a mild stroke, the earl's enthusiasm and energetic determination to expand his collection never wavered. His contacts abroad increased. Lord Edward Stanley Derby imported and bred more and more species, some now named after him bearing the suffix Derbiana or Derbianus; as well as the graceful, long-tailed Stanley Crane, originally from Africa. One gift from the famous American ornithological artist, J.J. Audubon, a pair of pigeons, bred so successfully that most of the flock had to be liberated to reduce numbers. Their cheeky descendants still plague the Knowsley and South Liverpool area.

Later in life, increasingly impaired hearing still did not prevent the earl attending the Zoological Society, presenting biological papers, communicating with collectors abroad and caring passionately for the burgeoning generations of his beloved specimens. He was providing employment for several managers and large numbers of estate workers, zoo keepers, veterinary scientists, secretaries, worldwide collectors and artists. By the time of the earl's death in 1851, at the age of seventy-six, his son, Edward Geoffrey Stanley, who was by then fifty-two, had already carved out a highly successful political career. He was acquainted with William Roscoe, the slavery abolitionist, and was the MP for Stockbridge in Hampshire (hence the renaming of the Cantril Farm/Knowsley district as 'Stockbridge Village'). The 14th Earl of Derby wished only to follow the path of his statesmen ancestors, not the footsteps of his naturalist father.

Almost immediately after his father's funeral, the new earl dispersed the inhabitants of the menagerie, presenting Queen Victoria with her choice of two Impeyan Pheasants. In less than six weeks, the rest were sold at auction, many to London's Regent's Park, some to the Zoological Gardens in Liverpool's West Derby Road, and some to private collectors. The projected Liverpool Museum (which eventually opened in 1860 on William Brown Street) accepted over 2,000 eggs, stuffed animals and birds. These eventually formed the nucleus of the museum's exhibits.

It wasn't until nearly a century later that the *18th* Earl found it necessary to find a new source of income in order to maintain the estate. Death duties (inheritance tax) had risen from 8 per cent in the nineteenth century, to 75 per cent at the end of the Second World War and finances became seriously depleted. In 1949, the 18th Earl, Lord Edward

David Ross (left), manager of Knowsley Safari Park, receives the Eden Award from Adrian Wills.

John Stanley, opened Knowsley Hall to the public. For five years, the entrance fees helped with the maintenance costs but it was soon necessary to reduce the size of the building by removing sixty-seven rooms and to be more enterprising in the use of the available amenities. The family moved into a smaller house and the main building was leased to Liverpool Council to be used by the Police Dog Unit.

In 1971, in an even more imaginative move, the 'Aviary' began its reincarnation as the Knowsley Safari Park, a joint enterprise between the 18th Earl and the famous circus owner, Jimmy Chipperfield. At first only a few acres were used, with an initial group of available animals. But the collection has grown steadily over recent years to include many healthy, exotic animals, including those great favourites the naughty baboons who would, given the chance, delight in jumping on to visitors' cars to play all kinds of 'monkey tricks'. To attract young children, extra amusements such as a carousel, a miniature railway, a sea lion show and falconry displays have been added. The Safari Park is once more under the sole ownership of the Earls of Derby. The present Lord Derby, the 19th Earl, has three young children, so he understands just what constitutes an exciting day out for all the family.

David Ross, who has been the managing director for the Safari Park since it opened forty years ago, has been its inspirational guiding light, introducing and caring for more and more species, adding to the comfort of visitors, voicing the friendly commentary that accompanies the wildlife drive, and furthering public relations superbly. He has added a lakeside farm so that very young children can go up close to baby animals. Adventurous daredevils appreciate his Aerial Extreme adventure course and for those who like creepy crawlies, David has created the Bug House, with snakes, lizards, spiders, etc. Before coming to Knowsley, he spent some years gaining valuable experience in Africa. While he was learning the ropes in Uganda, surrounded by all the turmoil of the early 1970s, Idi Amin drove into the campsite and asked if David could provide him with a pair of cheetah.

'I had to refuse. There were no such species in that area. Thinking back, I'm probably one of the few who have ever refused Amin and lived!' Hepatitis threatened his health in 1974, bringing his African career to an end, but he has been supremely happy on Merseyside, working hand in glove with the Knowsley Research and Conservation Team. He also has an artistic eye and produces a new free booklet every year, with delightful illustrations and information on all the amenities within the park.

What was once the exclusive home to a privileged minority now provides great fun, excitingly real education, exercise, social occasions for everyone, and, above all, a safe and nurturing environment for some of the world's most endearing creatures.

The present Earl of Derby and his wife, Lady Caroline, continue to take an active part in local life and in the Safari Park. In 2011 Lord Derby undertook a marathon sponsored cycle tour of Jordan, raising £35,000 for Willowbrook Hospice, St Helens, and Zoë's Place Baby Hospice, West Derby.

Charlotte Dod

1871–1960

Lottie – 'the Little Wonder'
Champion sportswoman and tennis sensation

Serena Williams, Gorgeous Gussie Moran, Martina Navratilova, all supreme tennis stars beloved by the Wimbledon fans. But how would their expertise have been affected had they been forced by protocol to wear long-sleeved, long dresses over several petticoats and with heavy drapery covering the waist and hips? The material would have been pure cotton or linen – much heavier than the man-made fabrics of today. Even worse, footwear was without sporting design, simply heavy leather lace-ups, such as anyone might wear for everyday walking.

The skimpy styles now in fashion on the tennis courts have evolved over the decades, owing much to the outspoken entreaties of Lottie Dod, the teenage tennis sensation of the 1880s. She complained that:

The ladies' dress is always a trial while taking exercise – and the blessings of our sex would be heaped upon anyone who could invent a more comfortable garment. As the skirt has to be endured [ladies were not permitted trousers anywhere] it is important to have it made somewhat short, reaching only to the ankles. It should be about three yards wide. If less, it would be apt to catch when one makes sudden springs from side to side, as in volleying. And, if wider, the wind will blow it about and make it hit the racquet when we try to drive the ball.

Suffering such unsuitable garments, Lottie's sporting achievements are even more remarkable, for she shone not only at tennis, she was also a consummate all-rounder, enjoying and excelling at golf, archery, hockey, ice-skating, mountaineering, cycling, sailing, tobogganing and curling. Can any twenty-first-century sportswoman (or man) beat that?

Lottie, the youngest of four siblings, did have one early advantage in life. She was born into a wealthy family and had no need to earn her living at any time. In later life, however, she did voluntary work in a Red Cross military hospital in Berkshire, during the First World War. She would willingly have gone to the Somme or Passchendaele but a long-standing hip problem prevented that. Her devoted service earned her a Red Cross medal in 1918.

Lottie's father, Joseph, a Liverpudlian cotton merchant, had become so prosperous during Victoria's reign, that he and his wife, Margaret, had been able to buy a fine property, with its own tennis court, Edgeworth, in Bebington, Wirral. Joseph Dod was happy to provide all his athletic children, Annie, Willy, Tony and Lottie with a comfortable home, the best quality sporting equipment and outfits for any exercise they cared to attempt, plus travelling and accommodation expenses all over the world. His rewards were the successes and fame that his offspring achieved and the honour they brought to the family. Far from adopting the life of the idle rich, all four went out into the world and strove to become the best in their chosen fields. Willy, in particular, matched Lottie in many of her activities and, in 1914, joined the Royal Fusiliers, surviving the war unscathed. He played tennis and chess to a high standard and won a gold medal for archery in the 1908 Olympics.

Financially, Lottie had no need to find a husband, the only guarantee in those days of security for most girls. So she didn't bother looking for romance and concentrated instead on the open-air life, testing her body to the limit and gaining thousands of fans as she won trophies and titles and set records from a very early age. In 1883, when only eleven years old she partnered her older sister, Annie, in the Manchester Tennis Tournament, the Northern Championships, losing out in the first round but winning the consolation tournament. Again with Annie, she won the Waterloo Tournament as well as the Ladies' Singles. In 1887, Lottie partnered the seven-times Wimbledon winner, Ernest Renshaw and, at the amazingly youthful age of fifteen, she won the Wimbledon Ladies' Singles. She is still the record holder as the youngest ever Wimbledon Ladies' Singles champion. Even with an imposed handicap, Dod beat Blanche Hillyard in the West of England Tournament and, in 1888, beat her at Wimbledon. In 1889, Dod won the Northern Open Championship but instead of entering Wimbledon that year, she and Annie went sailing with friends around the Scottish coast. But in 1891, 1892 and 1893, Lottie triumphed at Wimbledon, taking the title from Hillyard each summer. In doubles with Herbert Baddeley, Dod even beat her previous partner, Ernest Renshaw, as well as Blanche Hillyard's husband George Hillyard.

And there's more! In 1895, Lottie's brother, Tony, joined her at the Swiss winter sports resort of St Moritz. She passed the famous Ice Figure Skating Ladies' Test and, the following year, passed the Men's as well! She took part in the hair-raising St Moritz Cresta Run toboggan race, then went mountaineering with Tony in February 1896, conquering two mountains of over 4,000 metres. That summer saw Lottie and Tony on a long cycling tour of Italy and the following winter, she took her mother and Willy with her to St Moritz. This time, Lottie also competed in the ice curling event. Several Norwegian mountains were her next challenge, again with Tony, in the summer of 1897. Not content with this, Lottie then joined the pioneering new Women's Hockey Club in Spital, playing centre forward and becoming captain of the team. Every time Lottie played, the team won but if Lottie was elsewhere, the match proved a failure. In 1899, she became captain of Cheshire County Team, then played for England, winning the trophy against the Irish hockey team. Victory against Ireland came again in 1900, when Dod scored both the winning goals.

As if this wasn't enough, Lottie had been playing golf since she was fifteen. In 1894, she had helped to found the Moreton Ladies Golf Club, Wirral, also playing in the national championships at Littlestone, Kent. She reached the semi-finals in both 1889 and 1900. In 1904, she won the British Ladies' Amateur at Troon in Ayrshire making her the first and only woman ever to win both British tennis *and* golf championships. Sailing to Philadelphia, America, to attend the US Women's Amateur Golf Tournament as a spectator, only to find that a rule-change now entitled her to participate, she failed in the first round but took the opportunity to coax several top players to enter the British contest the following season.

Being a close-knit and loving family, the death of their parents brought much sadness to the siblings. In 1905, they sold Edgeworth and moved to Newbury in Berkshire. Lottie, Willy and Tony joined the Welford Park Archers. Both Lottie and Willy were selected for the 1908 British Olympic team with Willy claiming gold in the finals. After Tony married, Lottie and Willy reduced their sporting interests and moved to Bideford in Devon. Even into old age, Lottie still attended her beloved Wimbledon and it was while listening to the 1960 finals on radio that she died peacefully at the age of eighty-eight.

Brian Epstein
1934–67

The Fifth Beatle

During the Second World War, thousands of city-born British children were evacuated from their bomb-damaged home towns to the relative safety of country or seaside areas. Liverpool youngsters were sent to Southport or even further afield to North Wales. Some little ones were happy in their new 'foster' homes but many felt lonely, homesick for their real families. Often, evacuees were transferred from one environment to another, changing schools, missing large chunks of their education and causing them to feel either frustrated or abandoned.

Just such a one was little Brian Epstein, born in Rodney Street, famed for the many consultant and specialist doctors' consulting rooms there and also as the home of Victorian Prime Minister, William Gladstone (see *Liverpool's Own*). In Brian's memoir, he states, 'Evacuation to various parts of Wales and England during war years caused my education to be disastrously broken.' He attended Prestatyn Nursery School, Wales; Beechenhurst Preparatory School, Liverpool; Southport College; Croxton Preparatory School; Liverpool College (alma mater also to Rex Harrison, Noel Chevasse and Sir Simon Rattle – see *Liverpool's Own*) then Belvedere School, Liverpool; Beaconsfield School, Sussex; Claymore School, Somerset, and Wrekin College, Shropshire. Not all of these moves were due to evacuation as, owing to his lack of concentration and poor results, his parents were asked to remove him from several of the latter ones.

Brian's parents were Harry and Malka. As Malka is Hebrew for 'queen', Mrs Epstein was always known as Queenie. The family business was a furniture shop in the Liverpool suburb of Walton. Profits were good and the firm acquired several adjoining premises, then expanded into selling kitchenware and, in particular, musical instruments. One of their customers, Paul McCartney's father, once bought a piano there. The shop sign changed from EPSTEIN'S to NEMS, the acronym for North End Musical Stores.

Brian had no interest in retail, neither as a sales assistant, nor accountant, nor manager. At school he spent his Maths lessons doodling designs for theatre programmes. As a result, his marks were abysmal and he was considered to be of low intelligence and, consequently, developed a feeling of inferiority and hopelessness. He was asked to leave Liverpool College, but failed entrances to any major public schools, so was sent to a minor public school in the south, thus parting him once again from his parents and younger brother. The one thing he did embrace at these various upper-class educational establishments was good manners. He also developed a courteous and genuinely caring attitude towards his family, friends and everyone with whom he came into contact. An elegant dress sense was also nurtured. Brian cultivated a taste for the very best quality in all things. His appearance was always immaculate and, blessed with a ready smile, excellent hair and good deportment, he created a favourable impression wherever he went.

At sixteen, Brian told his father that he wanted to study art and become a fashion designer. Of course, his parents would have none of this and the teenage Brian was forced to sign on as an assistant at the family business. He hated it, in spite of showing early promise in powers of persuasion when, on his first day, a customer looking for a mirror left the shop having bought an expensive dining suite!

After a short stint in London, in 1952, as a clerical assistant in the Royal Army Service Corps, Brian returned north to work in the Clarendon Furnishing Shop, Hoylake, later returning to NEMS in Liverpool. But his heart was still elsewhere. He was a frequent visitor to the Liverpool Playhouse Repertory Theatre, developing a great admiration for one of the leading actresses, Helen Lindsay. She was tall, elegant, with expressive eyes and a beautifully modulated voice. After several months, Brian plucked up courage to approach her by letter. They met for afternoon tea. Brian showed a highly intelligent interest in all the productions at the theatre and, gradually, a genuine friendship developed. Helen explained all the behind-the-scenes effort needed for theatrical performances and, later, helped Brian to work on an audition piece when he applied for a place at RADA in London. Although he wasn't fully at ease as an actor, Brian was accepted. Soon realising that he didn't have the talent to become a star, he dropped out before completing his first year. London was an unlucky place for young Epstein. He once had all his valuables stolen, including passport, birth certificate, watch and cheque book. On another occasion, he was arrested and charged with homosexuality, which at that time was still against the law.

Back in Liverpool, Brian was appointed to a managerial post at NEMS Whitechapel, in the city centre. The record department, in particular, became a huge success and the young twenty-something realised that he had an administrative flair and a gift for dealing successfully with staff, suppliers and customers.

In his spare time, he still hankered after the bright lights of show business. In 1957, he applied to join the Playgoers' Club in Crown Street. This company had nurtured stars such as Leonard Rossiter, Rita Tushingham, John Gregson and Ken Jones, as well as Mildred

Spencer, drama tutor to Alison Steadman (see *Liverpool's Own*). That autumn, Ray Dunbobbin (see *Liverpool's Own*), later to star in *Brookside*, *The Liver Birds*, *Porridge* and *The Good Life*, had written a musical comedy set in a Parisian café. He had cast all the characters except the elderly proprietor. All suitable males were already engaged in other productions and Ray's opening night loomed ominously close. Ray auditioned Brian and took a chance on expecting such a young man to 'age-up'. With spectacles, false moustache and hair streaked with grey, Brian coped well enough to impress the *Liverpool Echo*'s culture critic of the time, Mary Ventris, and the show was a great success. Brian took small roles in other Playgoers' productions, notably an acted reading of a Chekhov play directed by Mildred Spencer.

In 1961, when Brian became the music columnist for the *Mersey Beat* magazine, he noticed references to The Beatles and The Cavern in Mathew Street. At the same time, customers at NEMS were ordering copies of 'My Bonnie' by the same group. As The Cavern was only just around the corner from Whitechapel, Brian called in to a lunchtime session. He remarked later, 'I was immediately struck by their music, their beat and their sense of humour on stage. When I met them, I was struck by their personal charm.'

This compliment could easily be returned to Brian by the Fab Four themselves, as they often admitted how highly they regarded him. As soon as he took over the personal management of their careers, they were happy to accept his advice on their image, dress and hairstyle and their toned-down language on stage. Brian's powers of persuasion and his tenacity were stretched to the limits when seeking a recording contract for his new protégés. None of the big companies were interested until, finally, EMI took a gamble on them.

Brian, himself, was a gambler. He also dabbled in drugs. He needed stimulants to keep up the hectic pace of his now all-consuming enterprise. As well as The Beatles, he also took on Gerry and the Pacemakers, Cilla Black and several other Liverpool groups. To The Beatles, 'Mr Epstein' became fondly known, in private, as 'Eppy'. When John, George, Paul and Ringo were awarded the MBE, they claimed it stood for 'Mr Brian Epstein'. The intertwined fame and fortunes of all five became a worldwide phenomenon. No other group has ever had so much written about them, nor become such universally recognised icons. Liverpool's tourism flourished enormously, thanks to Brian's vision, charisma, determination and business acumen, in creating The Beatles.

But the strain on his personal well-being took its toll. His use of drugs became more erratic and in 1967, he died of an overdose of barbiturates, aged only thirty-two.

Brian never married nor had children. His name and fame, however, live on in the recently refurbished and renamed theatre in Hanover Street, Liverpool; no longer known as the Crane nor Neptune Theatre, but now the Brian Epstein Theatre.

Lady Emma Hamilton

1765–1815

Amy Lyon
Emma Hart
Mistress of Admiral Lord Nelson

'She constantly reinvents herself', 'The Cinderella syndrome', 'From rags to riches' – how often do we read these clichés about modern beauties, pop-stars or film-stars? But the process from pauper to princess is not new and no-one could more successfully and speedily have risen from obscurity to worldwide fame and adulation (and back again) than little Amy Lyon from Ness on the Wirral Peninsula.

The story begins with Mary Kidd who, at the age of twenty-one, left her home in Hawarden, near Chester, and arrived in Ness in 1764, looking for work and a potential husband. Both were in plentiful supply, if only of lowly quality. Far from being the idyllic, rural Botanic Gardens, with the Merseyside postcode of L69, and elegant dormitory habitat of today, Ness was, at the time, a mining area, overrun with downtrodden young workmen. The hamlet was noisy and filthy with coal dust blowing about in the wind coming off the River Dee. Its tiny, ramshackle hovels were blackened by soot. The only gardens then were those where colliery workers struggled to grow a few meagre vegetables and keep a couple of hens or a pig. There were no bathrooms, toilets nor running water of any kind. Nevertheless, Mary quickly married the village blacksmith, Henry Lyon, and equally quickly gave birth to a daughter, christened Amy.

Working in the forge in unbearable sweltering heat was a great strain on the lungs and muscles. Henry needed vast amounts of liquid, usually home-made beer or gin and his long day and heavy drinking caused bad temper and a violent attitude towards his wife and baby. When Amy was only two months old, her father, Henry, died in suspicious circumstances. No record has ever been traced as to the cause of death. There were no registered accidents at that date and no evidence of any illness prior to Henry's death. Mary immediately left Ness, taking Amy back to Hawarden to be raised by the baby's grandmother. There, Amy had hardly any education and only the expectation of starting work at the age of ten. Amy was, however, extremely pretty, tall and slender with long, wavy, auburn hair, a fine complexion, rose-bud lips, good teeth and elegant, expressive hands. All this was unique in one so poverty stricken – poor girls usually had pallid or pockmarked skin, missing or rotten teeth, careworn hands and despondent posture. Amy had a lively and affectionate nature and she also had a good ear for music and a beautiful singing voice. However, she spoke in the local dialect with no knowledge of grammar nor correct ways of expressing herself.

Amy's first step on the route to escape from drudgery came when she was engaged as a maid for a doctor-surgeon in Chester. The doctor's library fascinated her and she improved her reading whenever possible. His daughter's sketch of the already attractive twelve-year-old still exists. Amy soon joined her mother in London and became nursery maid to another doctor's children. There she met another maid, Jane Powel, who later became a famous actress. London life went to the girls' heads – they stayed out all night,

sang on street corners and flirted with upper-class boys. Working in another musical household, with links to Richard Brinsley Sheridan and the Drury Lane Theatre, proved a beneficial influence on Amy's educational progress. Her personality was developing into one of caring and affectionate concern for those around her. She showed genuine love and sympathy for her employer's family, an attribute that never left her even in her later years. She also displayed natural intelligence and a great willingness to absorb knowledge, improve her education and adapt to her more exalted environment. She learned popular and classical songs and took on the etiquette, mode of speech and fashionable manners of her employers.

Moving into theatrical circles, Amy next became a maid to the actresses at Drury Lane Theatre, taking note of the musicality and choreography around her. Her beauty and appearance of perfect health and hygiene drew the attention of a charlatan doctor, James Graham. He had established a 'Temple of Health' where he beguiled wealthy, childless couples to use a 'connubial bed'. This delivered mild electric shocks, supposedly promoting fertility and conception. Amy, now a fully developed fourteen-year-old, was tutored as a model and dancer here, posing and swaying among arbors of flowers and a cornucopia of exotic fruits, all denoting health and fecundity. At this time she also modelled for the life classes at the Royal Academy of Art, in particular for George Romney. They became lifelong friends. His portraits of her, as various goddesses, nymphs, demure maidens and Shakespearian characters, often featuring her graceful hands, are numerous. Elisabeth Vigée Le Brun painted her in more revealing poses, ensuring that Amy's perfect figure was displayed to its best advantage. Frequently, Amy gazes at the viewer coquettishly, with chin lowered and eyes glancing sideways in a shy but alluring manner. Her fingers are often near her mouth or breasts.

From here, she was enticed into Madam Kelly's opulent bordello in Piccadilly, next to the now Ritz Hotel. Amy was one of the entertainers, with virginal singing and dancing while the aristocratic clientele perused the human 'menu' and chose courtesans to their taste. These sophisticated *demi-mondes* wore excessive cosmetics, ridiculously elaborate hairstyles and flamboyantly seductive gowns but Amy needed no powder nor paint and only the flimsiest drapery to display her natural charms. Among all this debauchery, Amy began to long for true love with a man she could trust and respect.

When Sir Harry Fetherstonhaugh 'bought' her out of Madam Kelly's establishment, Amy was delighted to escape. Her mother, now Mrs Cadogan, joined her and the two remained together until death separated them. Sir Harry took them to his sumptuous country house in the South Downs. He expected the fifteen-year-old to play both genteel hostess and saucy cabaret artiste to his many dissipated cronies. Amy, hoping to be kept on permanently in these gracious surroundings, tried to comply with his every wish. She stayed for more than a year learning to ride and to appreciate the fine art and expensive furnishings around her. The finest menus and wines were always served at the frequent banquets and gambling evenings. Amy began to develop her own style of entertainment, which she called her 'Attitudes'; poses and tableaux depicting female icons from Greek and Roman mythology, barefooted and draping herself only in silk shawls, as in the days of her modelling career. Here she met Charles Greville, singularly out of touch with the other wild guests, quiet, studious, self-effacing and highly critical of fox-hunting. Bored with the mindless toffs around her, Amy frequently found herself in serious conversation with Greville. Flattered by the attention of the teenage beauty, Greville fell in love with her and started to call her Emily. Unfortunately, she became pregnant with Sir Harry's child, who furiously abandoned her. Greville took her under his wing and persuaded her to give up her lively demeanor and to dress and behave like a nun, living in solitary confinement in his London home. This she willingly adopted, loyally obeying him with genuine affection and devotion. She expected to remain with him for the rest of her life, but Greville needed to find a rich and respectable wife. He persuaded Emma Hart, as he now called her, to visit his uncle, Sir William Hamilton, the British Envoy in Naples. Greville lied to both of them that this would be a long holiday only, while he went to Scotland on business. Eventually, in Italy, both the fifty-year-old Hamilton and the sixteen-year-old Emma realised the truth. Both were devastated. Emma, however, was truly grateful to the older man and a deep affection developed between them. With Emma's mother still in attendance, the marriage in 1791 was heartfelt and sincere. Emma, now Lady Hamilton, was welcomed into the highest society in Italy, becoming firm friends with Maria Carolina, Queen of Naples. Emma's dedication to self-improvement and education, coupled with her naturally sweet personality, guaranteed her popularity everywhere. Sir

William was besotted with his child bride and encouraged her to continue and develop more dramatically her 'Attitudes' to titillate his guests.

Meanwhile, Admiral Lord Horatio Nelson was gaining fame and adulation as the hero of the Battle of the Nile. An unlikely idol, he was short, very thin, scarred and sunburned, his grey hair was thinning, he was blind in one eye and had already lost one arm. But numbered among his thousands of female devotees, Emma Hamilton longed to meet this heart-throb. When he eventually visited Naples, such was her heightened state of anticipation that instead of a formal introductory greeting, she cried out, 'Oh, God, is it possible!' and fainted against him. As he was suffering from exhaustion after his battles, Emma nursed him personally and made no secret of her adoration for him. With a long-estranged wife at home, Nelson quickly fell madly in love with Emma. They remained faithful to their spouses for many months, but their mutual passion at last grew so overpowering that their infatuation became common knowledge. The ageing Lord Hamilton admired Admiral Nelson so much that he condoned the situation and the *ménage à trois* continued both in Italy and in London. 'Nelson Mania' broke out and the couple were fêted and followed by admiring crowds wherever they went. Every commodity possible bore pictures of the hero and the glamour girl. No murmur of criticism was ever heard.

Emma gave birth to Nelson's daughter, Horatia, and they both doted upon her, hoping to have a larger family as soon as possible. When the Admiralty eventually recalled Nelson to his ship, hundreds of letters of longing and desire passed between the besotted couple. When Sir William Hamilton died in 1803, Nelson and Emma assumed they could be together forever. While Nelson was away fighting the Napoleonic Wars, Emma did give birth to a second daughter who died within a few weeks. Nelson was killed at the Battle of Trafalgar in 1805. Emma, forbidden by the Admiralty to attend the state funeral, was utterly devastated and in her depression turned to drink and gluttony. The British Government ignored Nelson's wishes that Emma should be provided for, while her small inheritance from Hamilton was soon swallowed up by the maintenance of her London house and her wild spending. She aged prematurely, her auburn hair rapidly turning grey, too. She became fat and could no longer afford appropriate clothes. After spending a year in a debtors' prison, she fled with her daughter to France and died alone and broken in 1815.

Dame Rose Heilbron
1914–2005

Legally beyond

In America, the title of First Lady is only conferred upon a woman if she is the wife of the President of The United States. In Liverpool, during her highly regarded, distinguished and unique career, Rose Heilbron became the *first* lady several times over. Her own intellect, erudition and commitment were unsurpassed at a time when female barristers were rare in a man's world. Like Shakespeare's beautiful and brilliant defence advocate Portia, Rose was regarded as a 'wise young judge'.

Born in the early days of the First World War, Rose was the second daughter of Max and Nellie Heilbron. She attended Belvedere School For Girls in Liverpool, then Liverpool University, achieving a First Class Honours Degree in Law in 1935 and taking her Masters Degree in 1937. Her Bar Finals were so impressive that she was awarded the Lord Chief Justice Holker Scholarship at Gray's Inn, London, and was called to the Bar in 1939. In time, she was to become Gray's Inn Treasurer and Leader of the Northern Circuit. In 1940, she joined Chambers at 43 Castle Street, Liverpool.

Her expertise, dedication to detail and intricate preparation in every case served her well in court, giving her a confidence that matched and even outshone many of her more seasoned male colleagues. Some, envious of her rapid rise within the profession, hinted that she had unwittingly benefited from the fact that during the Second World War, some of the best male lawyers were absent on National Service. However, no-one could deny the expertise of this attractive, quietly but clearly spoken, even-tempered and above all knowledgeable woman. Her criminal and personal injury practice increased, her excellent reputation spread far and wide and she became well known to the public and a great favourite with the press. Indeed, in her post bag it was not unusual for her to receive proposals of marriage or requests for photographs of herself in a swimming costume. On a visit to America, she was fêted and treated like royalty by fellow lawyers.

Rose's actual marriage in 1945 to Dr Nathaniel Burstein was blessed in 1949 with a daughter, Hilary. 1949 was also the year in which Rose, after only ten years' Call, was included in Lord Jowitt's silks. In 1987, following in Rose's elegant footsteps, Hilary also took silk, much to her mother's delight.

In her long and distinguished career, Rose was famed for her numerous 'firsts'. She was the first woman to:

Take a First Class Honours Degree at Liverpool University
Take silk, jointly with Helena Normanton, both in 1949
Lead in a murder trial
Plead a case in the House of Lords
Be appointed a Recorder, followed by Honorary Recorder
Sit as a Commissioner of Assizes
Sit at the Central Criminal Court
Be elected Leader of a Circuit
Be Treasurer of any Inn
Be appointed Presiding Judge of a Circuit

Many sources include 'First High Court Judge' in the above list but, in fact, Rose was the second. Dame Elizabeth Lane preceded her in 1974.

Most of Rose's publicity came from her defences in notorious murder trials. In 1951, when Anna Neary was accused of murdering a woman in her bath, it was Rose who secured her acquittal. A year later Mary Standish, tried for the alleged murder of her husband, owed her freedom to Rose's defence. A footman at Knowsley Hall admitted shooting two men dead at the stately home, and gravely injuring Her Ladyship, the Countess of Derby, but Heilbron's clever move, to plead his insanity, saved him from the gallows. Her one defeat was in failing to prove the innocence of George Kelly, tried for the murder of the deputy manager during a break-in at the Cameo cinema. She was sure the conviction was unsafe. This was confirmed many years later in 2003 when Rose was eighty-nine years of age.

Rose was, herself, the personification of legal integrity.

Poetic Justice with her lifted scale,
Where, in precise balance, Truth with Gold she weighs.
Alexander Pope

Shirley Hughes OBE

Creator of Dogger, Alfie and a host of others

The life story of Shirley Hughes and her Merseyside connections would not be complete without some introductory words about her father, Thomas J. Hughes and his department stores.

Everyone on Merseyside will recognise the name of T.J. Hughes, the huge emporium at the top of London Road, Liverpool, and its many subsidiaries around the area. Like Mr Marks and Mr Spencer, young Mr Hughes started his working life with a market stall. His initial speciality was drapery but he soon expanded into other daily necessities and household goods. Using T.J. Hughes as his trading name, his one-man business was founded in 1912. Determined to make good, he worked tirelessly from morn to night. After a while he moved into a little shop and, by the time he was twenty-four, he was ready to take on greater challenges. When the firm of Owen Owen decided to move into premises in the very heart of the city, Thomas made them an offer to lease Aubrey House, their three-storey building, from them. Still working thirteen hours a day, with a nucleus of willing staff, Thomas's policy of stocking goods at extremely affordable prices became

highly successful. Many shoppers who were reluctant to venture into the more up-market emporiums in the city centre were happy to explore the bargains in the red-brick Victorian shop on the outskirts of the metropolis. By the 1920s T.J. Hughes had become a department store of some repute. The cash registers were never idle and eventually three more stores sported the name of T.J. Hughes. Thomas and his wife moved to a house in West Kirby on the Wirral Peninsula, and began to raise a family. As the town overlooks the nature reserve of Hilbre Island and has wide beaches, a marina and a long promenade, it is a great favourite with day-trippers from all around the region. These include artists and wind-surfers as well as families who like to walk out to the island at low tide.

By the time Dave Whelan bought the T.J. Hughes business in 1990, there were thirty-six stores nationwide. The value then was £42 million. In 2004, the chain was sold to Silverfleet and there are now fifty-seven outlets. In 2011, however, shoppers were shocked to learn that the business was facing administration.

One of Thomas' daughters, born in 1927, is Shirley, the renowned and much-loved writer and illustrator of books for young children.

'As a child born and brought up in a seaside town,' she says, 'with no television, only radio, my sisters and I pored over books and comics and surveyed the world from the flat roof of a garage.' She adds that much of her home-made entertainment came from dressing up and acting out plays to anyone who would watch, 'even the cats!' She also spent many happy hours drawing fantasy worlds. The local cinema was a 'terrific source of glamour' but so were the Victorian paintings in the Walker Art Gallery, Liverpool, especially as many of these are narrative art, depicting such scenes as weddings, shipwrecks or ancient legends.

However, 'Our quiet, well-conducted suburban childhood was interrupted by the Second World War. The grown-ups were far too absorbed in the war effort to bother about our educational, social or cultural achievements. I drew and wrote but kept it secret.'

She had a good high school education at West Kirby Grammar School, 'but I got out as soon as I could and went to Liverpool Art College and later the Ruskin School of Drawing and Fine Art, Oxford. I studied theatrical costumes and lithographic illustrations. The combination turned into a desire to illustrate stories. To me it was another kind of theatre.'

Initially, Shirley thought of becoming a theatrical set designer but she changed her mind after a brief try-out at Birmingham Rep. She moved to Notting Hill, London, met and married John Vulliamy, an architect and etcher, and started a family.

'I got the sketch book habit which has stayed with me always,' she continues.

You hang around observing and drawing real people, especially, in my case, children, then you go back to the drawing board and make it all up. The children in my books are not my own children nor other people's but inspired by a combination of both. When I first started going the rounds with a 'folio back in the 1950s, I got plenty of work illustrating other people's books, mostly in black and white. It was an excellent apprenticeship. As I had two small children, I tried my first own book, *Lucy and Tom's Day*, an unassuming little story about everyday life. I was very hesitant about colour then. It took a long time to let go and acquire the expansive confidence to let go and let it flow across the page. *Olly and Me* provided the opportunity to use the first person singular text in a kind of rhythmic verse form.

It was not long before Shirley had written more than fifty books of her own, with sales of over 11 million copies. She has also illustrated more than 200 others. Shirley's 1977 book, *Dogger*, about a lost toy, was the first to be widely published abroad and it won the Kate Greenaway Medal. In 1984, Shirley won the Eleanor Farjeon Award for services to children's literature while in 1999 Shirley was awarded the OBE and in 2000 she became a Fellow of the Royal Society of Literature. *Ella's Big Chance* was the title that won a second Kate Greenaway Medal for Shirley. This was in 2003, the same year that Liverpool John Moores University granted her an Honorary Fellowship. Liverpool University conferred an Honorary Degree upon her in 2004. At the seventieth anniversary celebrations of the Kate Greenaway and Carnegie Medals, *Dogger* was voted the favourite Kate Greenaway Medal winner of all time.

J. Bruce Ismay
1862–1937

Titanic *villain or scapegoat?*

There are many stories concerning the cataclysmic sinking of the *Titanic* but who among us knows the story behind the story? The actual event, its appalling consequences and senseless loss of lives have all been portrayed many times in books, films and television programmes but what of the man held culpable for this unprecedented catastrophe?

J. Bruce Ismay, an ill-fated figure of such magnitude that, had Shakespeare lived in the twentieth century, he would surely have availed himself of this disaster and its main protagonists to create another of his famous tragedies. It is an accepted fact that the bard's tragic characters, Lear, Macbeth, Othello and Hamlet, are intrinsically great and noble personages. Yet each have an underlying flaw which ultimately brings about their downfall and, in doing so, affects the fates of innocent people connected with them.

Like Macbeth, J. Bruce Ismay was an extremely ambitious strategist, an astute organiser and initiator of successful enterprises, involving many others dependent upon him for their livelihoods. But ambition was to prove his downfall, ruin the happiness of his wife, kill hundreds of blameless passengers and heap ignominy upon himself. Shakespeare did not offer any psychological reasons for the actions of his anti-heroes and it would be several centuries before Sigmund Freud put forward his theories about the child being father to the man. But by delving into the background of Ismay, it may be possible to discover the influences upon this initially well-intentioned but intrinsically flawed personality.

Born in Crosby, Merseyside, in 1862, the eldest son of Thomas and Margaret Ismay (née Bruce) Joseph Bruce Ismay was always known as Bruce. Thomas was descended from a long line of shipping magnates and was the founder of the White Star Line. He had built up a huge maritime empire, increasing yearly the number of ships built for him by Harland & Wolff in Belfast. He was a hard taskmaster within the company and a tyrant to his family and domestic staff. He always belittled J. Bruce and showed favouritism to his younger sons instead.

J. Bruce's first school was in New Brighton, Wirral, followed by Elstree School and Harrow, London. His education was completed by two years with a private tutor in Dinard, northern France. These long periods away from home naturally caused an emotional distancing and lack of warmth in family relationships. J. Bruce's nature, from infancy, was always sensitive and introverted. His father constantly berated and rejected him, making Bruce shy and ill-at-ease in company, thus giving a false impression of having a supercilious attitude. At an early age he started to make reckless decisions, such as borrowing his father's horse without permission, then galloping wildly across the Crosby, Formby and Ainsdale beaches until the horse stumbled, broke its leg and had to be shot. His father was furious, and the ensuing row damaged their relationship even further. While J. Bruce was still a boy, however, his father often took him to the company offices in Dale Street, Liverpool, during school holidays, to introduce him to the business side of running the White Star Line. Father and son both used the curved wooden hat-stand in the main office. At the age of eighteen, J. Bruce joined the company as a humble apprentice. Hanging up

his coat and cap as usual, he awaited his briefing for the day, then left. Shortly afterwards, a lowly clerk came to 'inform the new office boy that he is not to leave his clothes lying about in the Chairman's Office!' J. Bruce was so mortified at such an insult, from his father, he stopped wearing a coat at all.

But whatever his shortcomings, J. Bruce proved to have an ideal head for business and planning. His dealings with Harland & Wolff, the Belfast ship builders, went from strength to strength. The company expanded and prospered, creating more and more ocean-going liners and package steamers to carry passengers and goods all over the world. J. Bruce was sent as a representative to New York. There he met and fell in love with Julia Florence Schieffelin, known as Florence. On asking for her hand in marriage, J. Bruce was persuaded by her parents to live in America. J. Bruce gave his promise. The happy couple were wed in December 1888 and arrived in Liverpool eighteen days later! They did return the following February but only to a rented house on Madison Avenue.

Thomas Ismay's preferred younger son, James, completed his degree at Oxford and joined the company, working alongside his father in the Liverpool office. In 1891, both brothers were made partners in the firm of Ismay, Imrie and Company – a further slight to J. Bruce, in that he had not been promoted before his younger brother. This caused him to become even more withdrawn, taciturn and sarcastic. J. Bruce eventually returned permanently to England. Ultimately he and his wife had five children, one of whom died soon after birth. When old Thomas died in 1899, J. Bruce became head of the business. He certainly had a talent for administration. He was known as a perfectionist, unpopular with staff and colleagues, his shyness being mistaken for arrogance and callousness. Instead of vowing to distance himself from his late father's cold-hearted pomposity, it now became a situation of, 'The King is dead. Long live the King'. J. Bruce adopted his father's obsession with cleanliness and punctuality. While not an out-and-out Scrooge, Bruce became miserly in domestic matters yet donated grandiose sums to charities. Instead of a chauffeured car, he would walk or take the tram to his office. Yet, on seeing children in an orphanage playground on his way to work, he sent a personal cheque for £500 (worth at least £25,000 now), delivered by hand the same day.

Disability is no respecter of persons, however rich or high-born. J. Bruce was just such a one. He could not express in words his love for his wife and he found it totally impossible to give a public speech or talk to the press at any time. Instead he created a publicity department through which all information was routed. Reporters couldn't understand this, as old Thomas Ismay had always courted publicity and had an excellent rapport with all the local journalists. J. Bruce's antipathy with the media caused a rift with the American press baron, William Randolph Hearst who, after the *Titanic* disaster on 14 April 1912, conducted a personal vendetta against Ismay Junior, via his own newspapers. Headlines such as 'J. Brute Ismay' and 'Coward of the Titanic' vilified him unmercifully. Spin doctors and post-traumatic stress disorder counselling were as yet unheard of – although J. Bruce was in dire need of both.

J. Bruce Ismay's two huge mistakes were firstly in his financial planning estimates and secondly in not understanding the emotional devastation of those bereaved by the loss of so many human lives. The first of his disastrous mistakes was in the mindless decision to reduce the numbers of lifeboats to be carried by the *Titanic*. His reasoning was that 'too many' lifeboats would occupy deck space which could be better used as promenade areas for the many super-rich and titled first class passengers travelling on the *Titanic*'s prestigious maiden voyage. Nevertheless, these pitifully few lifeboats were still within the official guidelines. The numbers had never been upgraded to match the growth in capacity of recent liners. Ismay, now president and managing director of the White Star Line, saw himself as a thrusting entrepreneur, a visionary with innovative schemes for improving efficiency and pruning costs. He felt an obligation to increase profits for his shareholders and outstrip rivals such as Cunard. He studied other ships both in Britain and America and decided that the *Titanic* must eclipse all others as the epitome of luxury and prestige. He wanted every member of the aristocracy, every millionaire, every celebrity in any field to aspire to travel on board this unparalleled maritime palace. Every item, from chinaware and bedding to décor and entertainment, must surpass all rivals. A few extra lifeboats were not going to spoil the aesthetic beauty of the al fresco amenities. Nevertheless, certain parts and machinery were sacrificed to her sister ship, the *Olympic*, after its collision with a Royal Navy vessel, HMS *Hawke*.

Captain Edward J. Smith, a great favourite with the White Star Line, was engaged to command the *Titanic*'s widely publicised maiden voyage. It was he who boasted that she was 'unsinkable' and it was his words that were misinterpreted by his crew. When it became apparent that *Titanic* was doomed, he insisted that it should be 'women and children first' in the lifeboats but the crew took this as 'women and children *only*.' Even when the woefully meagre number of lifeboats were lowered, they were half empty, unnecessarily abandoning men who could otherwise have survived with their families.

J. Bruce helped to guide many passengers towards suitable lifeboats. When he could find no more to fill the last 'Collapsible C', realising there were still unoccupied seats, he and a first class passenger, William Carter, both jumped in just as it was being lowered. The fact that he saved his own life while the captain and so many passengers and crew lost theirs caused added grief for those traumatised by bereavement. It also provided sensational headlines vilifying Ismay in papers on both sides of the Atlantic. Florence Ismay, initially relieved at her husband's survival, found that he became even more unapproachable than ever. His nightmares were terrifying, he felt that God had forsaken him and he refused to acknowledge any blame for the disaster. The loss of his beloved ship seemed more personal to him than the deaths of so many of his fellow human beings. The only person to whom he felt he could turn for comfort was Marian Thayer, a beautiful first class passenger, whom he had met on board during the voyage. After such slight acquaintance, he assumed that, widowed as she was on that dreadful night, she could feel the same romantic feelings for him as he felt for her. In truth, the only affinity with him was the rapport she thought they both shared with all the other grieving survivors. They corresponded for a while until

J. Bruce Ismay (back, right) at the wedding of his younger brother.

she realised that she had been mistaken. She severed all connection and Ismay was left feeling even more isolated and outcast.

During the two courts of enquiry in Britain and America, Ismay failed to explain himself adequately. Scarred as he was by his unhappy childhood, his inability to give his wife the affection she craved and his total failure to empathise with other's emotions, this 6ft 4in giant could not defend himself against the probably trumped-up charges of pushing his way into a lifeboat ahead of others who later perished. Some accusations were made by people who could not possibly have identified him. He was in a boat with emigrant third-class passengers who spoke no English and, being permanently confined to lower decks, could have no idea who he was. Rumours and half-truths continued to surface around him but none could be proved. He was officially exonerated. Nevertheless, he took the brunt of the blame and was ostracised by friends. Later, he possibly had an affair with another survivor, Edith Russell, a fashion designer, who had defended him, saying his heroic actions had saved her life. Either way the damage was done. Ismay could not or would not speak up for himself and he descended into self-pity, all ambition spent.

He resigned his position with the White Star Line, bought a home in Connemara, Ireland, and disappeared from public life. Suffering from diabetes, in 1936, he underwent the amputation of one leg. His last years were spent in a small house on the Wirral peninsula but his death in 1937 was in Mayfair, London. His wife, Florence eventually renounced her British citizenship and returned to America. She lived with her sorrows to the age of ninety-two, dying in 1963.

Alan Jackson

Jackson of all trades
Radio Merseyside – Manx Radio
Roving reporter – singer – composer

Prescot born and bred, Alan Jackson credits his Mum and Dad, Edna and Les, with imbuing him with a strong work ethic and high moral principles. He fondly remembers his childhood visits to the Isle of Man, enjoying the beautiful scenery and the bracing fresh air.

'I consider the Isle of Man to be my spiritual home,' he says.

At school, he became head boy, keen on football, cricket and athletics. At the age of eleven, while on holiday, he started entering and winning talent contests for the under-eighteens. Out in the world for the first time, he became an apprentice in a printing firm, later going into retail and non-retail sales in North Wales. He says:

I've had such a wide variety of interesting experiences, mostly within radio broadcasting. I've met some of the most famous people in the world, from Dame Edna Everage to Martina Navratilova. I've even surprised Prince Charles as he walked into a studio, by presenting him with a 'Jolly Boy Award' for folks who have helped others in some way. There has been a lot of fun but, by strange coincidences, I've witnessed some dreadful and heart-rending catastrophes. For several years, I worked on the Isle of Man as a radio DJ and as a talk-show host. One evening in August 1973, after work, I went to visit an aunt who was on holiday from the mainland. She was staying in a hotel in Douglas, accompanied by one of her friends. We chatted and had an evening meal together. As I was about to leave, the friend looked out of the hotel window and commented that she thought she could see a wisp of smoke coming from further along the bay. Not taking much notice of this, I made my fond farewells and went out to my car. It was quarter to eight, it was drizzling and I was tired, so I just tootled along the road and eventually stopped to see what was going on at the Summerland Indoor Leisure Complex. It was a huge place with dance floors, games areas and several restaurants. On the passenger seat next to me there was a cassette recorder, a present from my mum. I picked it up for safety. I don't know why I got out and climbed all the concrete steps, but as I did, I noticed that the Crazy Golf ticket kiosk looked as if it had been alight and had collapsed against the wall of the main building. Suddenly, the double doors of the centre burst open. People poured out, screaming, tumbling over each other in their panic. Not knowing what was going on inside, I started to help people to get away from the building as quickly as possible. But there were hundreds and I felt that I was blocking the exit. So I moved away. Automatically, I

Alan Jackson on the Isle of Man.

Alan Jackson presenting his children's television programme.

switched on the cassette and spoke to some of the people passing me, asking them what had happened and who was inside. I didn't know what I could do to help. There were no mobile phones in those days so it seemed ages before any ambulances or fire engines arrived. A taxi driver had contacted his call-centre and some sailors out at sea had radioed in. There was pandemonium. Fire engines, helicopters, stretchers. So many people lost their lives and many more were seriously injured. Some children lost both parents. The silence when it was all over was eerie. The place looked as if it was made of burnt matchsticks. Apparently, young boys had been smoking and left cigarette stubs by the kiosk. Fate had brought me the world exclusive reporting of the Summerland disaster. But it was devastating. My memories are still so vivid but how I wish it had never happened.

Similarly at Heysel in 1985, although I wasn't actually involved, I was in Belgium at the time of the Liverpool v Juventus match. Being radio, our job was to provide a run-up commentary and suitable musical numbers before the kick-off. The shock of what actually happened, after the wall collapsed leaving 350 Italian fans injured or dead, was terrible. At the time, we had no idea of what was unfolding. When we realised, we were numbed by it all and the enormity of the disaster didn't kick in until a day or two later. The subsequent investigations discovered that the fifty-five-year-old stadium was in a poor state of repair with crumbling walls that had not been maintained for many years. All this in spite of the fact that Arsenal players and fans had complained years earlier but with no satisfactory result. It wasn't until 1994 that the stadium was rebuilt and renamed.

Recalling happier times, Alan mentions notable occasions such as commentating on the 1984/85 Charity Shield final between league champions Liverpool and FA Cup winners Everton at Wembley.

'In those days,' he says, 'It was known as the Friendly Derby because so many families had members supporting one or the other home teams. It wasn't unusual to see Reds and

Blues happily sitting next to each other.' Alan was also lucky enough to be commentating on the 2005 Champions League final in Istanbul when Liverpool ended the first half 3–0 down to AC Milan, only to fight back and win the match in the second half.

Alan is nothing if not versatile. As well as his long association with sport he has, in his early days, explored other avenues in show business. As a young Engelbert Humperdinck look-alike, he was a guitarist, singer and composer in his own right. Among his many hit numbers, during one of his favourite spells working on the Isle of Man, Alan penned the music and lyrics to 'Manxland'. With great pride and even greater humour, Alan reports that 'this went straight into the Port St Mary charts at number 145!' It must have been this that persuaded Radio Merseyside, at a later date, to promote him to Head of Music.

'Then there was the time when the Kop thought I was drunk,' continues Alan:

At various times I've been the announcer for either the Reds or the Blues. But way back in the days of Bill Shankly, the press box was positioned in such a way that the media folk, me included, couldn't actually see the pitch. We looked out onto a brick wall. The only way I could time my announcements to the fans was when the commissionaire signalled by waving his hand! As you can guess, this was far from satisfactory, often not synchronised with the action at all. Bill Shankly came to me and in his own inimitable way, said, 'See here, laddie. It would be a kindness if ye dinna break into an announcement just as ma boys are on the attack!' Then, when a new mike was provided, we didn't have time to test it. There was a kind of delayed action when I could hear my own voice playing back to me. So I slowed down my delivery to let the transmission catch up with me. What I didn't realise was that this made me sound slurring as though I'd had one too many. The whole Kop joined together to sing, 'What shall we do with the Drunken Sailor?'

Another of his gaffes was when the queen came to Merseyside to open the Garden Festival. She was just strolling past the press box when Alan whispered a comment upon her outfit to his colleague, sitting next to him.

'What I didn't realise was that the mike was open and she could hear every word I said! She wasn't best pleased, I can tell you.'

In recent years, Alan has hosted the popular 'Blue Chip' International Tennis Tournament in Liverpool's vast and elegant Calderstones Park.

'I must be the only Merseysider who has stood eye-to-eye with John McEnroe and lived to tell the tale,' he says.

From 2009 onwards, Alan has been proudly supporting his daughter, Amy, in every way possible, as she makes her way in the film and modelling industry. He is delighted with her success while so young and, along with her mother Rita, he has given Amy every encouragement.

'Of course she is beautiful,' he says, 'but she also has a wonderfully natural presence, and the tenacity to stay focused and deliver what's required of her. Beauty alone isn't enough. Nor always necessary. Look at another Liverpool girl, in the past. Rita Tushingham wasn't conventionally pretty. But she had presence and she worked hard at an equally early age. It goes back to what my parents taught me. It's self-reliance and your own determination that counts.'

Amy Jackson

Merseyside's own Bollywood film star

Every teenage girl's fantasy: 'One day, a film director will see my photograph and he will like it so much, he will phone me up and ask me to star in his next film. I'll do it and everyone will love it and I'll become an overnight success. I won't actually have to do anything. Just be myself.'

Of course, such dreams are ridiculous, they never come true. How could they? That's not the way show business really works! Let us take, for example, Amy Jackson, from Knowsley Village, Merseyside. At fifteen, Amy started to prepare for her GCSEs at St Edward's College in Sandfield Park, West Derby. The result was a very creditable eight good grades. Parents, teachers and Amy were pleased. Amy relaxed and began to think about life after school. The idea of modelling appealed to her but never having done any childhood modelling for catalogues or television commercials, she didn't know where to begin. Using her own initiative, she started to scroll through a few websites. She found the name of a highly respected agency in Manchester. She applied for an appointment and she and her mother, Rita, went to visit the main office. During the interview, it was mentioned that a workshop was planned for that very afternoon. Would Amy be prepared to try out at a moment's notice? Willingly, Amy agreed. Her mother went out for a little retail therapy and Amy joined the class. Before they left for home, Amy had enrolled with the agency. She took a course of lessons, posed for a portfolio of images and soon began to audition for modelling jobs. Realising that she enjoyed this kind of work, Amy again consulted the computer. This time she turned her attention to beauty pageants in the USA. After being chosen as Miss Liverpool, Amy decided to try America. Once again acting on her own initiative, she flew to America unaccompanied. In Texas, she won the competition and was crowned Miss Teen World.

Home in Merseyside again, Amy returned to photo shoots and publicity events. What she didn't know was that someone else was also searching through the websites. Indian film director, A.L. Vijay was looking for an English rose – but an English rose who would be acceptable to Indian audiences. Amy's long dark hair made her a suitable candidate and she was invited to go to London for an audition. She had to act out a scene and express various contrasting emotions. After this had been filmed, she was told that she was the most likely contender. She was pleased because she had always realised that a model's professional life is short-lived, whereas an actress can continue in the spotlight into her nineties if she so wished.

Assuming that her character, the daughter of the English Governor of India, would be a minor role, Amy felt quite relaxed. But when her contract was confirmed, that was when the hard work began. She had never seen a Bollywood film, so the director sent her some DVDs to study. Amy realised how much singing, dancing and even playing the piano was involved. When she arrived in India, accompanied by her mother, Amy was told that she would be starring with the very experienced twenty-eight-year-old Arya, already the leading actor in twelve hit films. She understood how famous he was when they were besieged by autograph hunters in a restaurant. Food was a slight problem for Amy. Although she likes Indian food, she found the 'real thing' rather spicy.

'I didn't think I could manage hot curries every night. Fortunately the caterers had made special arrangements for the British members of the crew and cast.'

After a few days to acclimatise, the hard work began. Amy had to take language lessons, as the dialogue for this film was in Tamil. She had already had to let her fake tan fade and now she was not allowed to sunbathe. Her extensions had to go, as the movie, filmed during the spring and summer of 2009, is a period romantic drama set in 1940. Constant rehearsals and dialogue tutorials became the order of the day. The script turned out to be almost a two-hander, with Arya and Amy in nearly every scene. The completed film opened to rave reviews and standing ovations in India and Amy was allowed to bring a one-night gala showing of *Madrasapattinam*, to Liverpool. All her family and friends were delighted to attend this unique occasion at the bijou Woolton Cinema in Woolton Village, Liverpool.

The studios of Southern India are actually known as Kollywood. Bollywood films are made in Northern India and it was there that Amy went to make her second film. It was a remake of the classic, *Vinnaithaandi Varuvaaya*. After all her hard but enjoyable work in the south, learning Tamil and studying the style and techniques required there, Amy had to start all over again in the north. The dialogue for this next film was entirely in Hindi and Bollywood films are a totally different genre. The acting is more flamboyant and the whole production is on a much more epic scale. Amy was more nervous than ever, especially as this director, Gautham Menon had cast Amy instead of experienced star, Trisha Krishnan.

'I'm not sure she will be too impressed!' said Amy, at the time.

Amy's most frequently asked question is whether she has any Indian ancestry. Amy replies, 'No, my mum is really fair and has blonde hair and my dad isn't dark either.' Amy and her mum spent Christmas 2010 in Mumbai and her dad, Alan, had a very important role, too. He paid for the flat but stayed at home to look after the dogs!

Between the two films, Amy had time to enter the Miss England finals. As well as the superbly elegant and classical, grey-beaded evening dress designed especially for her by LIPA graduate Charlotte Hudders, Amy sported a complete contrast in the 'Recycled' section. Again, designed by the ever-resourceful Charlotte, Amy's dress was an Indian-inspired creation of vibrant pink, purple, orange and blue vintage voile curtains, sent from Jamaica by Charlotte's cousin. Displaying the Indian-style bare midriff and with exotic make-up and hair jewellery, Amy was a stunning Indian version of a 'second-hand rose'. Charlotte had her own moment in the limelight when she graduated with a First at LIPA presented to her at the passing out ceremony by Sir Paul McCartney.

Amy's adventures in movie land have enabled her to take in the beauties of Kerala as well as the bustling city of Mumbai. Her next experience will include filming in America where the opening scenes of her third film are set. Initiative, hard work and self-reliance have certainly brought her good fortune and worldwide travel.

Sir Oliver Joseph Lodge
1851–1940

Science – Spark plugs – Spiritualism

Oliver Lodge was born in Penkhull, Staffordshire, the first of nine children. All these Lodge children displayed high intelligence and several of the siblings grew up to have distinguished careers. As well as Oliver himself, Richard was knighted for services to historical research, Eleanor became the Principal of Westfield College, London, and Alfred was a highly regarded mathematician.

The townships of the Potteries rely upon supplies of clay for the production of ceramic wares. Oliver's father, also called Oliver, was a ball-clay merchant and Oliver Junior's initial education was cut short at the age of fourteen when he joined the family firm as a travelling salesman drumming up orders for Purbeck Blue Clay. By the time he was twenty-two, his father had become successful enough to manage without Oliver, so the young man was able to study at the Wedgwood Institute, then become a student of Physics at the University of London. He graduated in 1875 with a BSc and in 1877 he became a Doctor of Science. He was an extremely popular figure in academic circles, impressively tall and slim, with an engaging personality and a warm tone of voice. All through his long life he always charmed his audiences with his amazing knowledge and his entertaining manner of discourse. In 1881, he was appointed as the first ever Professor of Physics and Mathematics at Liverpool University College, on a site previously occupied by a lunatic

asylum. From 1889 to 1893, he held the position of President of the Liverpool Physical Society. At Liverpool University, the present Physics Department and Laboratory are named after Sir Oliver Lodge and the Archive Department is trustee to numerous letters, diaries, photographs and newspaper cuttings chronicling his life and research. From 1900 until his retirement in 1919, Sir Oliver was the Principal of the newly founded Birmingham University.

Intellectually, Oliver Lodge was very much a man of his time. Scientific research was making huge leaps in the late Victorian and early Edwardian epoch. Bell, Edison, Darwin and Marconi were among those furthering knowledge in a wide variety of disciplines. Oliver's main scientific interests lay in his work in electricity, thermo-electricity and thermal conductivity. He furthered the development of a radio wave detector known as a coherer. This facilitated his breakthrough in radio signalling which he experimented with and tested in Liverpool. Although Marconi is always attributed with being the pioneer in this field, Oliver Lodge actually preceded him by twelve months. The Marconi company, in fact, bought a patent for Lodge's 'syntonic' tuner which allowed the frequency of transmitter and receiver to be verified easily and conclusively. Lodge was particularly interested in the detecting and generating of electromagnetic waves. At first he thought in terms of generating light waves as opposed to radio waves with their much lower frequencies but in 1894, he lectured at Oxford University to the British Association for the Advancement of Science, demonstrating the potential for transmitting radio signals. In 1894, he set up apparatus trying to detect radio emissions from the sun but this failed as his apparatus was not sufficiently sensitive. He was a polymath, branching out into literary publications on several occasions even while his inquiring mind was investigating many scientific theories. His experiments explored the nature of lightning, electrolysis, ether, the source of the electromotive force in the voltaic cell and he even wondered if fog or smoke could be dispersed by using some form of electricity. Present-day motorists are still benefiting greatly from Lodge's patent for electric spark ignition in the internal combustion engine. In every petrol-driven car, large, small, British or foreign, the spark plug, invented by Lodge and developed by four of his sons, is an essential component in the process of starting up the engine.

As well as his enormous academic, literary and scientific capacity, Oliver with his wife, Mary, were devoted to their family of twelve children – six sons and six daughters. In 1915, when their seventh child, Raymond, was killed on the battlefield, aged just twenty-six, the Lodges were devastated – they found it difficult to come to terms with the fact that such a young man had ceased to exist. In an era when numerous mavericks were setting themselves up as clairvoyants – visionaries with telepathic abilities – many bereaved families tried to make contact with loved ones who had 'passed on' to another life. Oliver had already shown some interest in this during the 1880s. He had joined the Ghost Club and had become President of the Society for Psychical Research and had studied the claims of an American 'medium', Leonora Piper, who had convinced him of the spiritual survival of the individual. In 1915, his preoccupation was again stimulated as he tried to communicate with Raymond. He met with Gladys Osborne whose work prompted him to write a book, *Raymond, or a Life After Death*. This man of science, who searched constantly for the true mechanism of the universe, was also intrigued by the claims of mind-readers, in particular the music-hall entertainer Irving Bishop. As many of

Lodge's contemporaries and colleagues were influenced by the writings of Charles Darwin, they were disappointed by this, as they considered it to be retrogressive hocus-pocus. But having investigated many pioneering theories about the nature of the universe, conducting research into the paranormal seemed perfectly logical to Lodge. Nor was he alone in these beliefs. Sir Arthur Conan Doyle was also a Ghost Club member and, after losing *his* son in combat, he also sought solace via spiritualism. Indeed, parents up and down the country frequently paid money they could ill-afford to charlatans who claimed to be channelling messages from 'the other side' to the grieving families left behind in this world.

As well as science, technology and literature, this polymath also took an interest in the politics of his era. He was a member of the socialist Fabian Society where he collaborated with George Bernard Shaw, Sidney Webb and Sidney Ball in writing and publishing *Socialism and Individualism*, and *Public Service versus Private Expenditure*. These were just two of the sixteen books he wrote and published.

In 1898, Oliver Lodge was awarded the Rumford Medal of the Royal Society and in 1902 he was knighted by King Edward VII. Stoke-on-Trent, the new name for Penkhull, granted him the Freedom of the City in 1928.

Before he died in 1940, aged ninety-one, Sir Oliver Lodge left written messages in sealed envelopes hoping to prove his theories but despite various attempts at contact via his suggested methods, all efforts were deemed inconclusive. His own philosophy is epitomised by his assertion that:

Death is not a word to fear, any more than birth is. We change our state at birth, and come into the world of air and sense and myriad existence. We change our state at death, and enter a region of – what? Of ether, I think, and still more myriad existence . . . in which communion is more akin to . . . telepathy . . . a region in which beauty and knowledge are as vivid as they are here and in which admiration, hope and love are even more real and dominant. In this case we can truly say, 'The dead are not dead, but alive.'

Colin James Paul McKeown

Television programme- and film-maker, producer, writer, director

'You should never ask anybody in the TV game if they have any anecdotes, particularly a producer because, given the slightest opportunity, they will pin you against a wall and recount anecdote after anecdote after anecdote and you would be lucky to escape without being bored to death!'

This was Colin McKeown's advice to potential journalists, biographers and authors.

Having travelled and worked in broadcasting all over the Middle East, heightened by plenty of Los Angeles and New York moments, underpinned by creating a soap opera in Kazakhstan and also filming the infamous Iranian Embassy Siege in London, you can see the scope of what you might be subjected to if I were to wax lyrical.

When pressed to expand on his feelings while filming the heart-stopping live action coverage of the West End siege, Colin explains:

I spent three years in the Middle East where my job was to train the indigenous Arab technicians in the use of the latest ENG technology. On my return to the UK in 1980, news-gathering was still in its infancy. Reporting had always been covered by film, so film cameramen were very cynical of this new video format. So much so that they would always insist on carrying a spare 16mm film camera in case the video broke down! However, their contempt was about to be expunged by one of the most captivating news events of the decade, the Iranian Embassy Siege. I was one of the chief ENG Engineers and, covering this episode, we all worked round the clock, using our ingenuity, helped by the versatility this new equipment gave us. As the police allowed some local residents access to houses near the embassy, we dressed a radio link engineer as if he'd just returned from holiday, with Hawaiian shirt, fake tan and a travel bag hiding a microwave transmitter. He managed to get a signal from the rear of the embassy to line-of-sight with the ITN Outside Broadcast vehicle. Within minutes of that link, we got the first pictures of the black-balaclavaed SAS on the rooftops behind the embassy. We made frantic phone calls via the ITN hotline to persuade the newsroom to put the signal out, live on air. They agreed and the pictures emerged just as the SAS swung round from the back of the building onto the balconies, providing the iconic TV news image of small explosives blowing the doors off, as the SAS team surged forward and disappeared into the upper floors of the building. My experiences in the Middle East helped me to organise this ground-breaking set-up and, two years later on 2 November 1982, the exact same cameras were also used to transmit the very first episode of *Brookside*, for which I also pioneered, in an electronic sense. The irony being that this Merseyside soap opera, shot in West Derby, Liverpool, had its technical roots in Saudi Arabia and also in London in very exciting circumstances.

Recalling other unique experiences while in the Middle East, Colin refers to his run-in with Colonel Gaddafi:

I was working in the south of Saudi Arabia in an area called Abba near the Yemen border, involved with broadcast training. Special permission was granted by King Khalid of Saudi Arabia as long as I was prepared to dress as an Arab. I could then legitimately assist the Saudi engineers in televising the Holy Pilgrimage of the Hajj. This is a ritual every Muslim aspires to undertake, at least once in their lifetime. I was able to use the broadcasting techniques I had acquired while working for *Match of the Day*, to record scenes in Mecca, by beaming signals to the transmitters at Jeddah. This was the first time the Hajj had ever been televised and therefore created a great deal of controversy. Being in charge of the whole operation, I was in the firing line of any polemics. Imagine how I felt to receive a phone call from Colonel Gaddafi, warning me and threatening me to stop all transmission as it was giving away aerial secrets for the very first time about the Holy City of Mecca. I explained that I was working for the Ministry of Information of Saudi Arabia and that the Royal Family of Saudi Arabia had approved the transmission of these signals. Gaddafi said he knew who I was and that I would never be welcome in Libya unless I cancelled the transmission immediately. Trying to calm the situation, I joked that he would never be welcome in Liverpool, particularly Huyton, if he harmed me. He paused only momentarily, then continued with his tirade of threats and aggression, only to be curtailed when one of the Saudi Princes took the phone from me and told Gaddafi, in no uncertain terms, what he could do with himself! As far as I know, Gaddafi has never been to Huyton and I have never had any yearning to go to Libya!

Born in Huyton, Colin attended St Aloysius School, Roby, and later Riversdale Technical College, near Otterspool Promenade, Aigburth, the latter being entirely thanks to Colin's far-seeing and enterprising mother.

My Mum was a typical Liverpool Mum, the major matriarch of our family. When I was a teenager, she gave me two options. 'You can either go to Butlins and sign on as a waiter, like a lot of your sad mates,' she told me, 'Or, I've got you a place at Riversdale Tech, to further your education as a TV technician. The choice is entirely yours.' Disillusioned as I was with school, I chose Butlins. 'That's the wrong choice, Son. You're going to Riversdale!' She made it quite clear that there was no point in arguing. Therefore, that was the start of *my own* chosen career! All of my career has been an absolute brilliant time, but if I were to pick out just two special periods. I would opt for one in the early days, in the mid-1970s, when I was learning my trade with probably the best film-makers in the world, especially as I was part of the team that produced the *Laurence Olivier Presents* series and the feature film, *Cat on a Hot Tin Roof* by Tennessee Williams, starring Natalie Wood and Robert Wagner. The second highlight for me came a decade later, starting in 1982, when I returned to Liverpool to co-create, with Phil Redmond, the groundbreaking soap opera, *Brookside*. It was a phenomenal achievement to be part of the development of this flagship show for the brand new Channel 4, as it was at that time.

Filming, as they did, in real locations, inside and outside real houses, in all weathers, rather than in little 'box' sets inside television studios, was so impressive that all other channels were soon forced to copy, as best they could, by building specially created open-air locations, streets, market squares and even whole villages. With Phil Redmond and Colin at the helm, *Brookside* also broke new ground with its story lines, dealing with sensitive personal issues, never before tackled by family-oriented, long-running serials. It was also the launch pad for the careers of many superb actors and actresses, some of whom Colin has been delighted to work with on subsequent projects. He was no stranger to soap operas, having previously worked on *Coronation Street*, *Emmerdale* and *Eastenders*.

Over the years, Colin has been the producer and executive producer on a wide variety of television genres and feature films.

'Every single title was a highlight,' he says with pleasure. Among the seventy-plus film and television titles, many of them with multiple episodes, with which Colin has been associated, either as writer, producer or executive producer, some of the most memorable are *In His Life: The John Lennon Story, Moving On, Nice Guy Eddie, Liverpool 1, Liam, Thief Takers, Damon and Debbie, The Real Eddie English*, and the ongoing series of

Justice, made at Colin's own film studio, LA Productions, based in Kirkdale, Liverpool.

As well as his Mum, Colin has also been blessed with a wonderful family, his wife Sara, daughter Gail, son Zachary as well as the late Billy, and also Larry, Donny, Maureen, Brenda, Lorraine, Anita and Corrine.

'If I included my nieces and nephews and extended family, it would fill the whole book,' he jokes.

Appreciating such good fortune, Colin wanted to put something back as a thank you to his home-town. More than ten years ago, he formed the charity of The Liverpool Film Academy Educational Charitable Trust, which does tremendous work in Kirkdale, North Liverpool, 'one of the most deprived areas in Europe'. His own company, LA Productions has also helped to revitalise the area, making use of the old St Lawrence School building, a centre for the community which helps residents with advocacy and legal services and provides suites for social and creative events.

'I feel fortunate to have an occupation that has been so varied and so satisfying,' concludes Colin.

Florence Maybrick
1862–1923

Did she murder her husband?
Was her husband a murderer?

It was quite a match . . . an attractive young girl, still in her teens, the daughter of an established, wealthy family, and an older man of even higher social status. *He* already had a mistress whom he had no intention of leaving. He continued with this long-standing affair even after his young bride discovered it. *She* had great charm and natural appeal and was popular with everyone who met her. Initially, she helped her husband to entertain his business associates, playing hostess at soirées, parties and formal dinners. *He* neglected her after she gave birth to their two children, often leaving her alone except for the domestic servants and the nanny. The unhappy wife eventually turned elsewhere to find the love, support and affection denied to her within the marriage. One of the ill-fated pair was doomed never to achieve a normal lifespan but died in such dubious circumstances that suspicions were aroused as to the involvement of the spouse in bringing about the other's death.

Sounds familiar? Then maybe you have previously heard some details of Florence and James Maybrick.

James, like many other Liverpool merchants in the nineteenth century, had made a fortune importing cotton from America. On one return sea voyage from the US to Liverpool, the forty-two-year-old broker had met a mother and her seventeen-year-old daughter on board. Both were social climbers – the mother's first husband, William Chandler, had been Mayor of Mobile, Alabama. After being widowed, Mrs Chandler had married Baron Adolph von Roques, a cavalry officer in the German army. On board the ocean liner, the daughter, Florence, lost no time in ensnaring James Maybrick, her senior by twenty-three years. They married in London in 1881 then returned to live in Battlecrease House in the Aigburth/Garston area of Liverpool.

All seemed well in the early years but James Maybrick was an iceberg – much of his secretive personality and lifestyle were hidden far below the surface. In order to prop up his middle-aged libido, he frequently took a cocktail of drugs. After his death, local pharmacists testified to the fact that he was purchasing regular supplies of arsenic, strychnine and other drugs considered by Victorian men to be aphrodisiacs. There were rumours that, as well as giving large sums of money to his favourite mistress, he had several others, with one of whom he had fathered five illegitimate children. This was in addition to his legitimate son James and daughter Gladys with Florence.

James was often away from home on business, in London or America. Florence felt neglected and depressed so she indulged herself in therapeutic spending sprees. James, meanwhile, had made the acquaintance of a Liverpool doctor who also travelled to London, mostly at weekends. They regularly shared a carriage and the doctor confessed to Maybrick that he needed human tissue for research purposes. It was always only during the trips to London by these two that the gruesome butchery by Jack the Ripper occurred – a strange coincidence. The evisceration of the corpses would be consistent with the need

to rip open the female torsos to remove internal organs, particularly the heart, possibly for scientific investigations.

Many theories have been put forward as to the identity of Jack the Ripper, some suggesting that Maybrick was the actual killer, but that this was on behalf of the doctor who, like Burke and Hare, needed the body parts for research purposes. The collaborative indications of this are the facts that a woman documented as 'Sarah Ann Robertson/Sarah Ann Maybrick, wife of James' (possibly indicating that she was his common-law wife only – or that Maybrick was a bigamist) lived in the Whitechapel area of London, hence Maybrick's familiarity with London districts. Secondly, a diary purporting to have been written in the nineteenth century came to light in 1992. In it 'Maybrick' confesses to the Ripper murders in great detail. It is also true that Jack the Ripper's serial killings came to an abrupt end in 1889, the date of Maybrick's death, and that some startlingly accurate details in the diary could not possibly have been known by any other than the Ripper himself or the police at the time. Authenticity, despite much scientific testing, has, to date, never been proven nor satisfactorily disproved.

Florence Maybrick, meanwhile, was eking out the meagre domestic budget allowed to her by her husband. She was a poor manager, often running up huge bills from local tradesmen, all the while squandering on fripperies. She created a vicious circle, pawning jewellery to buy necessities, and then gambling at the races in an attempt to win more money. She confessed by letter to her mother how terrified she was that suppliers might approach Maybrick in person, demanding that he settle her debts.

To add to her miseries, Florence's brother died in Paris and the Maybricks' son nearly died of Scarlet Fever. Maybrick's affection for Florrie dwindled to nil. He became violent towards her and even slept in a separate room. He threatened to change his will, leaving everything to their children and providing nothing for Florrie's old age. His behaviour became even stranger as his drug addiction increased. He still considered arsenic to be a pick-me-up, or rather a perk-it-up. Small though his self-administered doses were, they were addictive and had a cumulative effect upon his health which began to deteriorate visibly.

Naturally, when Florrie met a younger man, Alfred Brierley, also a cotton broker, she fell for him and began a blatantly open affair with him, flirting with him at that year's Aintree Grand National. This was possibly an attempt to make Maybrick jealous and therefore more affectionate. Ignoring all his own misdemeanours, he attacked her, tearing her clothing and giving her a black eye. Had it not been for intervention by their servants, he might have murdered her then. As a mediator, their doctor friend persuaded her to forget about Brierley if Maybrick paid off all her debts. They both agreed but both broke their promises.

Maybrick's health worsened as the increasing effect of so many years of bad living took their toll. Numerous doctors prescribed conflicting remedies, all to no avail. Maybrick had gastrointestinal disorders, headaches, lack of feeling in fingers and toes, general weakness and malaise. The medicines administered included Sal Volatile, jaborandi, cascara, morphine, prussic acid, iridium and henbane. With these and his years of small doses of self-administered arsenic, it is little wonder that he was in such a dire state of health.

At the same time, Florrie was also buying arsenic but in a different form. Fly-papers, long strips of sticky paper laced with arsenic, were much in use to trap and kill bluebottles in kitchens and sculleries. These, Florrie took home and soaked in bowls of water, to leach out the poison. This, she claimed was to use as a cosmetic device to improve her complexion, a common practice among ladies of the time. One of her maidservants noticed this and drew her own conclusions. She contacted Maybrick's brothers, hinting that Florence was trying to poison Maybrick. They took away all Florrie's authority, putting the nanny, Alice Yapp in charge of Maybrick's welfare. There followed accusations of Florrie sneaking arsenic into Maybrick's beef-tea. This she always denied. Maybrick died in 1889, only eight years after their wedding and Florence was arrested and tried for the murder of her husband.

At her trial, none of the medical witnesses could agree on the exact cause of death. There were so many substances found in Maybrick's body, his stomach was described as 'a druggist's waste pipe'. The judge allowed no mention to be made of Maybrick's long standing addiction, nor the fact that he had suffered from Malaria as a young man, treated at that time by strychnine.

An intercepted letter to Alfred Brierley proved that Florrie was still in love with him but it bore no hint of any malpractice as far as Maybick's condition was concerned. In fact, she seemed genuinely upset. It was only the servant's interpretation of her actions that implied guilt. When Maybrick fell into a coma, Florrie fainted. His death occurred before she recovered.

She was convicted of murder at St George's Hall, Liverpool, and was sentenced to death by hanging. Many lay people sprang to her defence and there was a public outcry. Eventually, her sentence was commuted to penal servitude for life. In fact, she served fifteen years. On her release, she returned to America, living in poverty until 1941, having reached the age of seventy-nine, but never having seen her children again.

Wilfred Owen
1893–1918

First World War poet

The date of Wilfred Edward Salter Owen's birth, on 18 March 1893, in the closing decade of the Victorian era, and of his death, twenty-five years later, on 4 November 1918, in the final week of the First World War, immediately give strong hints to the external circumstances of his short life. In expressing his inner thoughts and emotional struggles, his poems have probably done more to indicate the turmoil and horror of warfare than any political speeches or flickering newsreels of the time.

Born in Oswestry, Shropshire, the eldest of four children, Wilfred's parents were Harriet and Thomas Owen. Their comfortable, middle-class existence owed much to Wilfred's grandfather, who provided their home, Plas Wilmot. But on his death in 1897 the family had to move to Birkenhead where Thomas Owen found work with a railway company. For schooling, Wilfred attended Birkenhead Institute and later Shrewsbury Technical School.

Wilfred's mother was a genuinely devout evangelical Christian, who encouraged her children to follow a pure and dedicated path towards salvation of the soul, embracing a genuine concern for others. Wilfred's bond with her was deeply affectionate and respectful. As she was not physically robust, Wilfred grew up often taking responsibility for his younger siblings' welfare. He was a bright and conscientious pupil, particularly interested in Botany, Music, French and, above all, classical and romantic poetry. Unable to win a scholarship to Oxford, Cambridge or the University of London and too poor to afford the fees, he travelled instead to a village parish near Reading, where he became the vicar's assistant and an auxiliary teacher at Wyle Cop School in Shrewsbury. Here, for the first time, he witnessed real poverty, unemployment and deprivation. Contrary to his previous views, the first seeds of disillusionment against the cynical attitudes of authority were now sown.

A happier period was to follow. Between 1913 and 1915, Wilfred lived and worked in Southern France as an English language tutor at the Berlitz School in Bordeaux. Here he was contented, greatly appreciating the beauty of the area. His caring, artistic and pious nature blossomed.

In these idyllic surroundings, his life seemed totally remote from the impending doom of the First World War but gradually the news items seeped into his consciousness and conscience. Despite holding strong pacifist views, he felt compelled to return to Britain. He enlisted in the Artists Rifles Officers Corps, trained at Hare Hall, Essex, and was commissioned as a Second Lieutenant, Manchester Regiment. Back in northern France, in very different circumstances, the first of his 664 letters to his mother (all preserved for posterity) seemed light-hearted and full of hope; although he realised that he differed dramatically from the men in his command, many of whom relished the brutish hostility of battle and were accustomed to rough, primitive conditions at home. Within a very short time, however, the tone of his letters changed completely, confessing, 'I can see no excuse for deceiving you . . . I have suffered the seventh hell – I have not been at the front, I have been in front of it . . . in a dug-out in the middle of No Man's Land. We had a march of three miles over a shelled road . . . to where the trenches had been blown flat out . . . The ground was not mud but an octopus of sucking clay, three, four, five feet deep, relieved only by craters full of water.'

In poetic form, he expressed it:

> Bent double, like old beggars under sacks,
> Knock-kneed, coughing like hags, we cursed through sludge,
> Till on the haunting flares we turned our backs
> And towards our distant rest began to trudge.
> Men marched asleep. Many had lost their boots
> But limped on, blood-shod. All went lame, all blind;
> Drunk with fatigue, deaf even to the hoots
> Of tired, outstripped Five-Nines that dropped behind.

The brutality of war soon became more personal when a trench mortar blew him off his feet onto the already rotting corpse of another soldier. Surrounded by gun-fire, the screams of the wounded and the piteous cries of the dying, he realised that the only way to cope with such terrors was to deaden one's own feelings, denying all natural instincts:

> And some cease feeling
> Even themselves or for themselves
> Dullness best solves
> The tease and doubt of shelling . . .

Gas attacks, mortar attacks, a huge gun, fired at least once every minute, snow impacted by fierce frost, all conspired to deny proper sleep. Abysmal food, inadequate clothing and sparse medical supplies intensified the horrors. And still they had to fight on. Death was a merciful release. Wilfred just could not reconcile himself to his duty as a patriot with his revulsion at the carnage around him. He drove himself to lead his men bravely, while hating with every ounce of his being the very acts of war he was compelled to undertake. One letter to his mother tells her that he is 'a conscientious objector with a very seared conscience.'

He forced himself to become oblivious to danger. His whole concentration was now upon the strategy of war and the determination for victory.

He wrote to his friend, the poet Siegfried Sassoon, 'I cannot say I suffered anything; having let my brain grow dull . . . My senses are charred.'

But all the physical deprivation, added to the mental torture of his revulsion of what he witnessed, began to play on his psychological welfare. His whole being was torn apart. He wanted to refuse to kill – it was against his religious principles – but he felt he mustn't opt out. That might be an act of cowardice and he must prove himself worthy of his ideology. His entire existence, corporal and spiritual, was rent by trauma. He was diagnosed with shell shock, repatriated to Craiglockhart War Hospital, Scotland, and thence to Northern Ireland for convalescence. Part of his rehabilitation was to teach for a few months in a normal high school, followed by a posting to Ripon, where he wrote many of his bitterly anti-war poems.

On his return to the front in 1918, he was sent to lead the men of the Second Manchesters in their attacks on the village of Joncourt, to rout the enemy ensconced there. Strangely, he now felt at one with men in his command, those men who had seemed so different from him when he first joined up. In a letter to his mother he stated, 'Of this I am certain: you could not be visited by a band of friends half so fine as surround me here.' In another letter he claims, 'I am more and more a Christian . . . Suffer dishonour and disgrace, but never resort to arms. Be bullied, be outraged, be killed, but do not kill.'

Added to that was the fact, shown in his early poems, that he had already taken the step from heterosexual love . . .

> A maid
> Laughing the love-laugh with me; proud of looks . . .
> Her heart
> Quivering with passion to my pressed cheek . . .

to homosexual love:

> In that I loved you. Love, I worshipped you,
> In that I worshipped well, I sacrificed
> All of most worth. I bound and burnt and slew
> Old peaceful lives; frail flowers, firm friends; and Christ.
> I slew all false loves, I slew all true
> That I might nothing love but your truth, Boy.

Now taking the painful step from pacifist to warmonger, Christianity versus patriotism were tearing his very soul asunder – the conflict within was more terrifying than the battles without.

One line of Owen's typifies the contradictions and lunacy of what Robert Burns called 'Man's inhumanity to man'.

'I am the enemy you killed, my friend,' was Owen's way of expressing the oxymoron.

Although victory for the allies was obviously in sight, the Germans, with machine guns, still held the east bank of the Sambre-Oise Canal. In order to cross the canal and capture this contingent, Owen's men began to construct a pontoon bridge. May were hit by enemy fire. Owen, at the front, as always, was killed outright. Total victory and an end to the war was declared exactly one week later.

In Shrewsbury, where Wilfred's mother was now living, the church bells, silent all through the war, were clamouring out their celebratory message of Armistice Day on 11 November 1918, when, answering the knock on the front door, Wilfred Owen's happy and excited mother received the telegram announcing her son's death.

Posthumously, Second Lieutenant Wilfred Edward Salter Owen was awarded the Military Cross for bravery. The citation read:

> For conspicuous gallantry and devotion to duty, in the attack on the Fonsomme Line on October 1st/2nd, 1918. On the company commander becoming a casualty, he assumed command and showed fine leadership and resisted a heavy counter-attack. He personally manipulated a captured machine gun from an isolated position and *inflicted considerable losses on the enemy*. Throughout he behaved most gallantly.

The psychological journey from a pious, sensitive, academic pacifist to heroic but soulless, amoral warrior was complete.

Sir Alastair Pilkington
1920–95

The glamour and practicality of glass

Glass has existed since time immemorial. Long before man discovered a method of making it artificially, nature had created glass when lightning had struck sand. Once man devised a way of manufacturing and shaping this substance, it became an all-important and highly prized item. There is evidence of a form of glass used in Mesopotamia 3,000 years BC.

The Romans in Britain, during the first century AD, produced ornate vessels, mosaic tiles and a form of window glass. With the spread of Christianity, monasteries and churches greatly valued their stained-glass windows. The glass-blowers of Ancient Greece realised how precious their secrets were. Determined to preserve their monopoly at all costs, they had ways of keeping spies silent. Anyone caught divulging any information, however insignificant, was either killed or sold as a galley slave, never to return to their homeland. In 1695, William III of England introduced a tax on windows. So, many homeowners bricked up several windows per house, in order to evade paying the inland revenue. The act was only repealed in 1851.

For many centuries, glass has been and still is one of the most widely used and versatile of man-made commodities in the world. It is functional, decorative, non-toxic and recyclable. It can be sturdy or fragile according to requirement, transparent or any colour under the sun, brittle or fibrous. Spectacles can improve vision, patterned glass can provide privacy. It can imitate precious jewels, help to celebrate weddings, sporting triumphs and business success. More mundanely, it can keep refrigerated milk fresh. We take it for granted but it is essential to every part of our lives.

In the late seventeenth century, Crown Glass became widely used in domestic windows. Because it was blown, the usual shape was a small square with a 'bull's eye' in the centre. Many squares were needed to form a complete window. These allowed light into the building but effectively prevented anyone looking through into the interior.

In 1826, a partnership was formed between three Lancashire families, the Pilkingtons, the Bromilows and the Greenalls. They began to manufacture glass suitable for windows and called themselves the St Helens Crown Glass Company. The Pilkingtons were the most dedicated to the business and, when the last of the Greenalls left in 1845, the name was changed to Pilkington Bros, becoming, in 1894, Pilkington Bros Limited.

It was an era when glass-making burgeoned. In 1860, Pilkington and their nearest rivals, Chances of Birmingham, had nine furnaces each. They were just beginning to export when companies in America started their own companies. Other British firms succumbed to the competition but Harry Pilkington (1905–83) had become the only manufacturer producing sheet, rolled, plate and cathedral glass. He instigated numerous innovations and improvements in efficiency so that costs were cut. By the end of the 1920s, Pilkington was considering abandoning sheet glass but a development of a continuous flat-drawn process completely changed his mind.

By 1935, Pilkington developed the 'twin' machine to grind both sides of the ribbon of glass simultaneously. This gave the company international advantages. Subsequently,

Pilkington allowed overseas businesses to use this process under licence from the parent company. For many years, Pilkington was the biggest employer in St Helens.

Young Alastair Lionel Alexander Bethune Pilkington was born in 1920. He was educated at Sherborne School and then graduated from Trinity College, Cambridge. While he was still a student, he was called up during the Second World War. He was taken prisoner of war in Crete and held in captivity for three years. This period of inactivity did at least give him the opportunity to concentrate on ideas for improving scientific practices. At the end of the war Alastair married Patricia Nichols (née Elliot) and they eventually had a son and a daughter. In 1947, Alastair joined the family firm.

Between 1953 and 1957, Alastair and his colleague, Kenneth Bickerstaff, worked with a team of scientists in an attempt to improve the glass-making process. It took seven years of long and often disappointing experiments before they were satisfied with their results. They needed support and finance from the company. This was only possible because of the autonomy of a private, family-owned firm. Many people questioned the worth of such a programme, but they were eventually able to invent the Float Glass Process, a revolutionary method of high-quality flat glass production, by melting floating glass over a bath of molten tin, thus avoiding the costly process of having to grind and polish plate glass to make it clear.

Their subsidiary, Triplex Safety Glass, became a worldwide supplier of toughened and laminated glass for cars and buildings. In the next decade, father and son used the royalties generated by float glass to create franchises in Argentina, Australia, Canada and Sweden.

By this time Harry Pilkington's business acumen and his general interest in twentieth-century culture had brought him to the attention of MPs and to the hierarchy of the BBC. Now Sir Harry, he was invited to chair an all-party inquiry into the state of broadcasting in the UK. In particular, the committee was requested to investigate the potential development of commercial radio stations around the British Isles. Controversially, after much research and analysis, the committee reported that the public had already shown that commercial *television* was unpopular, especially as it showed too many American Westerns and crime stories. Therefore commercial *radio* was totally unnecessary and would be a waste of resources. In truth, the members of the inquiry were of the wrong generation. Young people certainly did want a different form of radio than that provided by the BBC. It was this unwelcome decision that prompted the launching of so many off-shore pirate radio stations, especially Radio Caroline, piloted by the up-and-coming DJs of the hippy era.

Alastair was also highly thought of. He became a Director of the Bank of England, Pro-Chancellor of Lancaster University and Chancellor of Liverpool University. He was a director of BP, British Rail and the Wellcome Foundation and became a Fellow of the Royal Society. In 1970, he was knighted and he became the Chairman of Pilkingtons in 1973. With enormous reserves of energy, he still had time between all of this to indulge in his favourite sports of skiing, paragliding and sailing. Nor did he forget others. He set up the Community of St Helens Trust and raised funds for the Cambridge Foundation. Pilkington has continued to benefit St Helens to this day, by charitable organisations for all sections of the community.

One unexpected sideline to the Pilkington industry came about when it was discovered that the warm water from the factory, discharged into the nearby canal, was beneficial to a certain form of wildlife. Someone had the bright idea of releasing tropical fish into the canal. These flourished, prompting legendary stories of cross breeding and hybrid creatures swimming around the perimeters of St Helens. Maybe there should be a glass version of the sculpture of the Little Mermaid or something similar reclining outside St Helens World of Glass.

William Henry Quilliam
1856–1932

Sheikh Abdullah Quilliam
Haroun Mustapha Leon
Henri Marcel Leon

Here was a man with an enquiring mind, a man who devoted much contemplation and scrutiny to comparative religions and whose studies and practical work helped to influence public thinking and guide many others seeking expression in their spiritual quest.

William Quilliam was born and brought up in Fairfield Crescent, Liverpool, bordered on one side by Newsham Park and on the other by elegant bowling greens. His parents had moved to this desirable Victorian address from the Isle of Man. Robert Quilliam, William's father, was a wealthy watchmaker at a time when gold fob watches and half-hunter watches with their hinged casings and heavy gold chains were very much the 'must-have' status symbol of every gentleman in business or society. Ladies, too, wore watches, as an item of jewellery, often pinned to the bodice of evening dresses by delicate filigree chains.

The family were Methodists by religion, appreciating the joyful hymn-singing and the simple, abstemious lifestyle. As the years passed, William began, instead, to attend

the ministry of the Revd Charles Beard, a prominent Unitarian preacher, whose creed does not acknowledge the Trinity, but believes in one unique God. William was a pupil at the Liverpool Institute for Boys in Mount Street (now the Liverpool Institute for the Performing Arts). During his 'gap years', before and after studying for his Law degree at King William's College on the Isle of Man, William travelled to the south of France, Algeria, Tunisia and Morocco. While in Morocco, he was greatly impressed by the natural beauty of the Atlas Mountains, the exotic architecture of Marrakech and, above all by the spiritual lifestyle of the Mohammedan people. At the age of twenty-two, he joined a Liverpool law firm and began a very successful career as a solicitor. In 1879 he married Hannah Johnstone with whom he had a family of three sons and five daughters. He was a conscientious and popular advocate. While still in practice near the Liverpool Police Courts in Dale Street, William continued his interest in the Islamic faith, taking holiday visits to North Africa to further his studies there.

In 1887, William converted to Islam and was granted the name of Sheikh Abdullah Quilliam. He joined with Mrs Fatima Coates to publish two monthly magazines, *The Crescent* and *The Islamic World*. On Christmas Day 1889, he established the Liverpool Muslim Institute at 8 Brougham Terrace, West Derby Road. It became England's first mosque. In 1891, William took one of his sons to Constantinople (Istanbul) to help him to understand the Islamic faith. William also helped his mother and his own children to convert to Islam. In 1896, he created a home for orphaned children in Shiel Road, Liverpool, and called it The Medina. He was an intellectual whose debates were of great interest to scientists and scholars. He travelled widely and received support and honours from leaders in the Islamic world, among them his title of Sheikh and the position of Persian Vice Consul to Liverpool.

In 1908, Quilliam decided to leave his practice in Britain and live in Turkey. His son sold the building in Brougham Terrace and it became an office for the registry of births, marriages and deaths. Lacking the impetus of Quilliam's leadership, the Muslim community on Merseyside dwindled. On returning to Britain in 1914, it was at Onchan, Isle of Man, that he settled, adopting the French name of Henri Marcel Leon or, using the same initials, sometimes Haroun Mustapha Leon. He died in London and is buried at Brookwood Cemetery, near Woking.

The Abdullah Quilliam Society, formed in 1996, is raising funds to restore the building at Brougham Terrace in order to reopen the historic mosque and create an educational centre. In 2008, the Quilliam Foundation was established to reintroduce the moderate and tolerant aspirations advocated by the Merseyside man who was so highly esteemed in the Islamic world.

Eleanor Florence Rathbone
1872–1946

Daughter of a dynasty – determined democrat

The name of Rathbone has resounded through the ages in the history of Liverpool, North Wales and indeed the whole of Britain. Highly regarded as Eleanor Rathbone is – being commemorated by the building named after her at Liverpool University (the Eleanor Rathbone Building now houses the Department of Sociology, Social Policy and Criminology as well as the School of Psychology) and by the Chair of Sociology carrying her name (currently held by Professor Sandra Walklate) – Eleanor's genealogy bears great importance in the forming of her character and the manner in which she responded to the social and political circumstances of her era.

Being born during the reign of Queen Victoria, living through two world wars and witnessing the political upheavals and injustices in both Eastern and Western Europe, Eleanor took no heed of her own life, except as a means to help others in danger or in poverty and deprivation. Blessed with admirable tenacity and insightful compassion for those exploited or victimised, Eleanor was a genuine humanitarian. She was the first female to come to prominence in a long line of high achievers and philanthropists, all named William Rathbone.

The first William Rathbone of note came to Liverpool from Gawsworth, near Macclesfield, in 1730. He felt that commerce in Liverpool offered better opportunities due to its worldwide connections in the shipping trade so began to build up a successful business on Merseyside and his sons and grandsons developed the enterprise into the following century. This was during the height of the infamous slave trade but William Rathbone the third and his sons were diametrically opposed to the nefarious activities of their fellow merchants. They refused to deal with any companies who built slave ships or were involved in any way with the slave trading triangle (see William Roscoe in *Liverpool's Own*). While each generation of Rathbones prospered and expanded, this was not at the expense of their work force. The Rathbones were benefactors, genuine in their Unitarian and Quaker faiths and always striving to use personal wealth for social reform and educational opportunities for those less fortunate.

In long-standing family trees, the branches sometimes wither or succumb to contamination; but successive Williams had the good judgement to choose wisely when falling in love. Consecutive Mrs Rathbones were intelligent, diligent and had equally high aspirations as their husbands, concerning the welfare of others. All were treated as equals by their husbands and the power behind the throne never diminished. Each generation was able to build on the heritage of the previous, both in business concerns and in the good they were contributing to the community. In time, William the fourth owned a sawmill, became a ship owner then ship builder, cotton trader and a merchant banker. William the fifth's political endeavours were directed against bribery and corruption in public life.

William Rathbone the sixth, the father of Eleanor, lived from 1819 until 1902. He and his brothers continued trading as general merchants under the name of Rathbone Bros & Co. They prospered and expanded, William marrying Lucretia Gair in 1847. However, after giving birth to their fifth child, Lucretia became ill. William engaged Mrs Mary Robinson to nurse his wife at home. William had already become aware of the deprivation abounding in Liverpool and he had witnessed the cholera and dysentery epidemics that had killed thousands of immigrants who had fled the Irish Potato Famine in the 1840s. He had helped to fund Kitty Wilkinson's efforts to bring sanitation and hygiene to the poverty-stricken 'courts' where the orphans and widows huddled together in their thousands (see *Liverpool's Own*). Watching the devoted care and comfort given to Lucretia by Mrs Robinson, William was struck by the contrast between this and the total neglect of destitute women with similar health problems in other parts of the city. When Lucretia died in 1859, he asked Mary Robinson to continue in his employment but to go out to the poorer areas to teach hygiene and the rules of healthy living. After  a month, 'She came crying to me, saying that she could no longer bear the misery she saw.' He asked her to continue to the end of her three-month contract. At the end of that time, 'She came back saying that the amount of misery she could relieve was so satisfactory that nothing would induce her to go back to private nursing.' This decided him to extend the service but found that there were not enough trained nurses. The education was disorganised and of poor quality so in 1860, he wrote to Florence Nightingale for advice. Florence suggested the establishment of a training school attached to the Royal Infirmary. Within three years, William had the organisation ready to invite students. A long-term correspondence and friendship with Florence Nightingale ensued, with many of the letters preserved for posterity.

William persuaded his wealthy women acquaintances to finance district nursing in their own suburbs. They also took on the roles of supervisors. Although charitable, this was non-sectarian and soon Manchester, Derby, Leicester, Dublin and London's East End followed this example. When William became an MP he set up the Central School of Nursing in Bloomsbury.

William the sixth continued to plough personal wealth into projects to help the poor, such as the construction of two open-air convalescent homes and the improvement of medical care in workhouse hospitals. Education was also of great importance to him and he helped to found the University of Liverpool and the University of Bangor, North Wales.

William remarried in 1862. In time, he and his second wife, Emily Lyle, had a further five children. Emily was a highly intelligent and resourceful woman, eager to embrace the principles and philanthropic endeavours of her husband. On taking his seat in Parliament in 1868, William took his second wife and burgeoning family with him to London, leaving his widowed mother in charge of the family home in Liverpool. Thus it was that their penultimate child, Eleanor, was the only one of her siblings not actually born in Liverpool. In honour of her father's regard for Florence Nightingale, Eleanor was given the middle name Florence.

In infancy, she had a succession of nursemaids and private tutors before going to Kensington High School, London, and she completed her education at Somerville College, Oxford, where she studied Roman History, Moral and Political Philosophy, Logic and Greek History.

She had inherited all the determination and humanitarian dedication of her Rathbone ancestors and was encouraged to live a life committed to the welfare of others. Female students, at that time, were deprived of many of the normal privileges afforded to male undergraduates. Eleanor bore these constraints with decorum but took advantage of one activity which was frowned upon but not forbidden. She took up smoking. At that time smoking symbolised the independent spirit of intellectual young ladies. For Eleanor, it became a lifelong habit, sometimes more important than eating. More than once she forgot whether she had breakfasted or not. Fashionable clothes were of little interest to her either, although she was never eccentric in appearance.

What she did notice, however, was the deplorable conditions under which some sections of society were expected to work and the inequality of women's financial role within marriage. Determined that this should not continue, she made a report to the Poor Commission in 1903 detailing the results of an enquiry into the labour situation in the Liverpool Docks. In 1909, Eleanor became the representative for Granby Ward, Liverpool. No woman had ever previously been elected to the Liverpool Council. With the advent of the First World War, Eleanor co-ordinated the Association for the Families of Soldiers and Sailors, to ensure the distribution of funds to relatives of servicemen. She also realised the problems of mothers who struggled with little or no income, even though, in some cases, the husbands had cash to spend on drink or gambling. She hated the fact that women's contribution to the economy was undervalued. She felt that their role as mothers was paramount to the development of succeeding generations. If they did work outside the home, they were paid less than male colleagues doing exactly the same job. From as early as 1917, Eleanor began campaigning for some kind of allowance to be paid directly to mothers of young children. Although it was many years before she achieved her goal in this respect, she never lost sight of her crusade.

Price 1d.

THE FAMILY ENDOWMENT SOCIETY

UTOPIA CALLING!

Miss E. F. Rathbone, M.P.

A Plea for Family Allowances from an Address Broadcast by Miss Eleanor Rathbone, M.P., from Northern Stations on February 11th, 1930

In 1929 Eleanor became the Member of Parliament for the Combined Universities. She stood as an Independent, just as she had on the Liverpool Council. This typified her whole ethos – always true to her causes yet always fiercely autonomous. As an MP she was able to command more respect but there were still many who could not subscribe to her views. During the Depression of the 1930s, she continued to push for extra benefits for underprivileged children, especially in the provision of cheap milk. She won re-election to the House of Commons in 1935, despite a proposed threat that the university seats might be abolished altogether.

By 1938, Eleanor could see the peril looming on the Eastern European horizon. Recognising the threat of another world war, she joined the British Non-Sectarian Anti-Nazi Council, attempting to protect human rights in Czechoslovakia as well as Austria, Germany and, ultimately, possibly Britain. She was already campaigning on behalf of the increasing number of potential refugees and was utterly opposed to the policy of appeasement advocated by the government – Chamberlain's 'settlement' with Hitler was anathema to her. She rightly predicted that Hitler would break his hollow promises of not attacking the rest of Czechoslovakia, in return for the Sudeten northern frontiers. She regarded the Munich Agreement as a betrayal. Like Cassandra, in ancient mythology, she had the gift of prophesy but, again like Cassandra, no-one would believe her predictions. There was a massive exodus of panic-stricken refugees from Eastern and Central Europe and Eleanor and her colleagues spent hours lobbying, phoning, writing letters and pressing Chamberlain to ease restrictions on entry to Britain.

Not only were there too many barriers to displaced persons trying to enter Britain but, erroneously, some foreign nationals already living and working in Britain for many years were classed as enemy 'aliens' who should be interned. The government was blind to the fact that most of these people were actually the *victims* of the Nazi regime, terrified of Hitler and hating everything he stood for. Many were highly intellectual and had been working as doctors, scientists and lecturers for the good of the British population. A newly built but as yet unoccupied housing estate in Huyton, Liverpool, was commandeered as a temporary camp – helpless individuals were arrested and transported from all over England to these unfurnished shells, surrounded by barbed-wire and military guards. The education of some, as young as sixteen, was interrupted. The boys were made to sleep in tents in the little back gardens of the terraced houses (see *Liverpool's Own*). Food was appalling and these well-meaning, pro-British but highly distressed academics felt just as threatened as their compatriots back in Nazi Germany. Eleanor took up their cause, doubling and trebling her efforts, actually visiting the inmates to assure them of her best endeavours. Even so, most were transferred to similar conditions on the Isle of Man and then shipped to the icy winter of Canada. It was at least eighteen months before Churchill's government saw the light and revoked the internment rules but Britain lost the benefit of some of these brilliant brains as they chose to remain in Canada.

Eleanor had not forgotten her own compatriots and she was still determined to achieve equal rights for the working class and the unemployed, particularly women. After all, she had lived through the suffragette era and had had to stand up for her own rights and those of her personal friends. Her campaign for Family Allowances finally triumphed in 1945, under the Attlee government.

She had served under three prime ministers and enhanced the already esteemed name of Rathbone. Although she never married nor had children, her name lives on. In addition, her cousin Elfrida worked tirelessly for children's rights. John Rankin Rathbone served as MP for Brecon from 1935 until he was killed in the Battle of Britain in 1940. His wife Beatrice was then elected in his place. The Rathbone flag was still carried by Eleanor's great-nephew, Tim Rathbone who became MP for Lewes from 1974 to 1997 and, in 2011, her great-niece, Jenny Rathbone, was elected to the National Assembly for Wales as the representative for Cardiff Central.

Roly and Rust

Of the Wildlife Trust and the National Trust

The twins Roly and Rust are just two of the dwindling colony of red squirrels who inhabit the Lancashire and Merseyside region. They live mostly in the pine woods of Formby and in the areas close to Ainsdale beach and sand dunes. The beautiful conifer copses and the fine white sands at Victoria Road, Formby, are protected and managed by the National Trust. The squirrel population is monitored and cared for by the Lancashire Wildlife Trust.

Animals and humans have inhabited the shores of Liverpool Bay and the Sefton Coast since prehistoric times. The evidence for this can occasionally be found in the footprints, preserved by nature, in the silt beds along the foreshore. Relatives of Roly and Rust have also set up home further afield, some at Southport's Hesketh Park, some inland at Rufford and Ormskirk and others along the coastline at Crosby and Blundellsands.

The word *squirrel* is derived from the ancient Greek word 'Skiouro', meaning shadow (skia) and tail (oura). Roly and Rust's ancestors had virtually no predators and they enjoyed an idyllic high-life in the tree-tops of north-west Britain, using their bushy tails as parachutes and rudders to assist their flight-like jumps from branch to branch. Pine cones and nuts were plentiful and the climate was reasonably stable. Squirrels build nests, called dreys in the crooks of branches, thus providing a firm foundation in case of windy weather. They sometimes play 'cuckoo-in-the-nest' by 'squatting' in ready-made nests, in bird boxes, under the eaves of thatched roofs or even in church towers. Contrary to popular belief, squirrels do not hibernate but they do store away enough food to last through the winter. Their bright red coats fade slightly in autumn, becoming dull enough to cause them to be mistaken for their cousins, the grey squirrels. But the reds have tufted ears and are smaller in size than the greys.

It was only with the development of modern civilisation that the tranquillity of the landscape began to be disturbed. Squirrels in general retreated to the seclusion of islands such as Skye in Scotland, the Isle of Wight and Brownsea Island in Poole Harbour. But Anglesey, Wales, is not suitable for them due to the road bridge allowing 'invasion' from the mainland. The greatest threat to the health and happiness of the native British red squirrels came with the introduction of the American grey squirrel in the early twentieth century. The greys trespassed and took over in broad-leafed forests and then started advancing into coniferous areas as well.

In January, 2009, tragedy struck at the Merseyside population of red squirrels. An epidemic of squirrel pox infested the area and workers at the Lancashire Wildlife Trust feared that the popular little creatures might be in danger of extinction. Conservation Officer, Fiona Whitfield, explains:

> Grey squirrels are immune to the virus but they are carriers, passing it on to the reds. It's most distressful to the little creatures as the symptoms are similar to pneumonia or the dreaded myxamotosis. It causes swollen and runny eyes, lesions on paws and genitals; the animals suffer from extreme thirst and they keep cleaning themselves excessively. We were all very worried.

In spite of scientific research by graduates such as Tim Dale Phd and staff at the Red Squirrel Survivors Project, it is still unknown how the disease is transferred. The RSPCA workers at Stapeley Grange have been setting humane traps, then attempting to treat the infected individuals. But the disease is, so far, proving resistant to all types of medication. Fortunately, the epidemic stopped short of Hightown, Blundellsands and Crosby. Total numbers, however, shrank by 80 per cent and the situation looked bleak. However, by October 2010, Fiona was able to report an improvement. New sightings at Formby were a happy surprise.

> After a long period of limited sightings, it was a delight to see three reds in ten minutes. In addition, at Mere Sands Wood Nature Reserve, the first reds since 1998 were noticed and there have also been glimpses at Halsall.

By October 2011, there was a significant improvement in the population although not reaching the original numbers.

The beguiling appearance and elusive behaviour of squirrels has long fascinated human beings. The Edwardian children's writer and illustrator, Beatrix Potter realised this when she created her fictitious Squirrel Nutkin. In the twentieth century, the cartoon character Tufty helped young children to take care on the roads and to be aware of the Highway Code. Hopefully, in the twenty-first century, humans will be able to aid the local reds back to full health and happiness so that their future will be assured for all time.

David Stuart Sheppard

1929–2005

Bishop David Sheppard – Baron Sheppard of Liverpool

By the time David Sheppard was ordained into the Anglican ministry in 1955, he was already a world famous cricketing star, having captained England against Pakistan in 1954 and, previously, as an undergraduate at Cambridge, having set a record of 3,545 runs in 1953. Good looking, good natured, good sportsman and good company, he was greatly admired both on and off the pitch, but his modesty and concern for the good of others never wavered.

Born in Reigate, Surrey, in 1929, where his father was a successful solicitor, David showed early promise, both academically and at sport. It was at Sherborne School in Dorset that his skill on the cricket pitch and his intellectual ability were both recognised. His years as a student at Trinity Hall and Ridley Hall, Cambridge, were preceded by his military service as a second lieutenant in the Royal Sussex Regiment. While still a student, he met the love of his life, Grace. Their long and happy marriage brought them a daughter, Jennifer.

David played for Cambridge from 1950 until 1953, scoring records of 1,281 and seven centuries. He also scored two double centuries for Cambridge and a third double century for Sussex. He was named a Wisden Cricketer of the Year for 1953. During the following three years, he devoted more time to his church studies, but in 1956, he joined the winning team in the Fourth Test against Australia at Old Trafford.

David was ordained as a deacon in 1955, becoming a priest in 1956. Over the following two decades he worked tirelessly in Islington, Camden Town, Woolwich and Peckham, always involving social and educational projects, helping the unemployed, the needy and the elderly. At the same time, he was still providing sporting thrills for his thousands of cricketing fans. In 1962/63, his parishioners were happy to allow him to join the tour to Australia. Naturally, he spent his Sundays Down Under as a guest speaker in the cathedral cities visited by the England team. Such was his popularity that every Anglican cathedral 'from Perth to Brisbane' was filled to capacity. At Melbourne, he made 0 and 113 in the

victorious Second Test but any catches he dropped were jokingly pounced upon by team-mates Richie Benaud, Bill Lawry and Neil Harvey, with skits such as 'Pretend it's Sunday, Reverend, and keep your hands together!' Even David's devoted wife, Grace, joined in the fun. When an Australian couple pleaded to have their baby christened by the sports idol/vicar, she laughingly warned that David might drop the infant! David, of course, took it all in good humour.

In 1969, David was ordained as the Bishop of Woolwich in the Diocese of Southwark. He was often invited by

the BBC to speak on topics concerning unemployment, poverty and housing problems. He campaigned tirelessly for social reform and better understanding of the causes of petty crime. In recognition of his inner-city ministry in the East End of London, David's appointment as Bishop of Liverpool seemed a natural progression. He was warmly welcomed and became an integral part of Merseyside life, settling with his family in West Kirby, Wirral.

When his daughter, Jenny converted to Catholicism, Grace and David showed sympathetic understanding and the family harmony was not disturbed in any way. Indeed, David was determined to improve dialogue and aspirations with his colleagues of all denominations. Only a year after his appointment, he was consulted by the Papal Nuncio in Britain, as to the cultural and spiritual needs of Merseyside, prior to the appointment of Derek Worlock, in 1976, as the Roman Catholic Archbishop of Liverpool. These two became great friends, co-operating in the advancement of ecumenical compatibility and uniting in their common concern for urban regeneration, especially after the Liverpool riots of 1981. David often disapproved of Margaret Thatcher's policies and was co-opted onto the Archbishop of Canterbury's Commission for Urban Priority Areas. Naturally, as a sportsman himself, he had heartfelt concern and sympathy for the victims of the 1985 Heysel and 1989 Hillsborough disasters. He joined his friend Derek Worlock to search for ways of bringing some comfort to the bereaved families.

The two were inseparable. So close were they that they often officiated at joint ceremonies or deputised for each other if the need arose. They could read each other's thoughts and sometimes completed the other's sentences. In true Scouser fashion, they earned the affectionate nickname 'Fish 'n' Chips' because they were always in the newspapers together.

In 1994, both David Sheppard and Derek Worlock were honoured with the Freedom of the City of Liverpool. Among other privileges, this included the right to shepherd their sheep down Bold Street in the city centre. Neither used their entitlement literally but both guided their human 'flocks' towards a righteous path and an amicable vision of unity within the community. Their efforts, along with other denominations, were instrumental in pulling together a city which could so easily have become divided in its sporting, political and religious loyalties – to such an extent that in the run-up to Liverpool's European Capital of Culture year, one of its proud claims was Faith in One City.

David has two autobiographies, *Parson's Pitch*, charting his twin careers of cricketer and priest, and *Steps Along Hope Street* referring metaphorically to his pilgrim's progress, also acknowledging the geographical link between the Anglican and Catholic cathedrals. It has always been a significant fact that the Anglican cathedral was designed by the Roman Catholic Sir Edward Lutyens while the Metropolitan Catholic cathedral's architect was the Protestant Sir Giles Gilbert Scott.

In the New Year's Honours of 1998, David Sheppard received the life peerage title of Baron Sheppard of Liverpool, in recognition of his indefatigable efforts towards secular and spiritual regeneration. As he had retired from the ministry, he now took his seat on the Labour Benches in the House of Lords. Completing the circle of sport and spirituality, in 2001 he accepted the invitation to become President of Sussex County Cricket Club.

David was the only person to play, in his youth, at Lords and to take his seat in the Lords in his more mature years.

Fritz Spiegl

1926–2003

Musician, humorist, polymath extraordinaire

Scouse – 'By a bewk, ref!'
English – 'You have forgotten the rules of football, Mr Referee !'
French – 'Vous avez oublié les regles de foot, Arbitre!'
German – 'Du kennst die regeln nicht, Schiedsrichter!'

Scouse – 'Amoraite, ta'
English – 'No thank you' (i.e. I'm all right)
French – 'Non merci'
German – 'Nein danke'

From *Scouse International*, the sequel to *Lern Yerself Scouse*, both by Fritz Spiegl (each phrase also has a Japanese translation).

Fritz Spiegl always claimed that he wasn't 'born' until 1939, when, at the age of thirteen, he arrived in England as one of the Kindertransport refugees from Nazi Germany. By this, he indicated his immense gratitude to Britain for the welcome he received, the education from which he benefited and the happy life he was fortunate enough to live in this democracy. In actual fact, he was born in Austria, near Haydn's birthplace and on the anniversary of Mozart's birthday.

'Hitler shook the tree, an apple fell to earth in Britain, it later ripened into a musician, journalist, Liverpudliologist, broadcaster, composer and publisher,' said Walter Cook, the New York writer. The multi-talented Fritz said that, 'Hitler's coming and my arrival in England changed my life and turned me into an Englishman.'

He and two other refugee children were looked after by Captain (later Lord) Margesson, who was at that time Secretary of State for War. He and his American wife taught Fritz English and educated him at Magdelen College School, where he learned 'rugger and how to yawn politely without opening the mouth.' After hearing a girlfriend play the flute, he took it up at the age of sixteen and then won a scholarship to the Royal Academy of Music. His first job was with the Royal Liverpool Philharmonic Orchestra, where he later became principal flautist and stayed for many happy years.

Fritz recalled that he hated Liverpool for the first six weeks but then fell in love with it. He settled in Toxteth, married his first wife Bridget Fry and had three daughters, Emma, Julia and Helen. As well as his family and Liverpool in general, Fritz's second wife, Ingrid, says:

Fritz loved living near Princes Park but was annoyed when the 'fashion' for stealing cars and dumping them, burning, into the park lake, was in vogue. The gates were left open twenty-four hours so, after much complaining, asking for them to be locked, to no avail, he took matters into his own hands and welded them shut. Instead of prosecuting him, the local authorities made him an 'honorary park keeper' with his own set of keys, and put padlocks on the gates.

Alongside his musical career, Fritz developed other talents and interests. He branched out into journalism, contributing to the *Guardian, Liverpool Daily Post, Telegraph* and *BBC Music Magazine*. He worked with BBC Radio on programmes to bring classical music to a wider audience, he organised fun concerts with titles such as 'Nuts In May', 'Midsummer Madness,' 'April Fool's Concert', 'Liszt Twist', and 'Concerto for Car and Orchestra'. Some of these were so outlandish and haphazard that, on one occasion, the accompanist played one piece of music but the soloist sang something completely different.

His love of all things British included a fascination with the English language, including the idiosyncrasies of certain phrases such as 'He isn't up yet,' meaning exactly the same as 'He isn't down yet.' He compiled *Contradictionary: An A-Z of Confusables, Lookalikes and Soundalikes*, listing thousands of words such as 'transport' which can be pronounced two different ways to change it from a noun to a verb. Similarly, 'bow' with two pronunciations and three different meanings, or 'cord' and 'chord' sounding the same but having no connection in meaning. Also included were phrases with a common meaning, as in 'split personality', 'Jekyll and Hyde', and 'schizophrenia'. He loved puns and *double entendres*, calling one of his books *The Joy of Words: Bedside Book for English Lovers* and another, *Keep Taking the Tabloids: What the Papers Say and How They Say it* and another *MuSick Notes: A Medical Song Book*. Two more scholarly books were *An Illustrated Everyday History of Liverpool and Merseyside* and *The Lives, Wives and Loves of the Great Composers*. His two most popular books are his own self-published (i.e. printed, published and marketed from the cellar of his own home) *Lern Yerself Scouse* and *Scouse International*.

Lern Yerself Scouse translates everyday Liverpool phrases into the kind of English understood outside Merseyside. For example, 'Wossadoo, la – wuz yer judy lyin' on yer shairt?' actually means, 'Why are you late for work this morning?' Meanwhile 'Am skint, lennuz a meg,' means 'Could I borrow a small amount of money?' 'Didjer gerrennywur?' means 'Were you successful with your new girlfriend?'

Fritz's two favourite charities were Médecins Sans Frontières and the Salvation Army, as he admired all the practical good they do. Like every true Scouser, however, he himself was quite prepared to do a little wrong for the sake of the greater good. As Ingrid reports:

Pre-1989, when the Berlin Wall came down, Fritz was visited by the distraught wife of a fellow musician. The couple had been on tour behind the Iron Curtain when the husband had been hurt in an accident. While still in hospital, his visa ran out, so he was trapped, while she was allowed out of the country. Knowing Fritz's ingenuity, she turned to him in desperation. Fritz rang a stamp-making firm in Liverpool and eventually got a rubber stamp made, which was smuggled to the friend who, with the appropriate ink and a lot of nerve, doctored his documents, got out of the country and was reunited with his wife.

His first wife Bridget pays tribute to Fritz, saying:

He was a wonderful man who thought that everyone had special gifts; he admired our plumber and joiner and wanted to learn from them just as much as from the great musicians and writers. He said he would do everything he had done, even if he wasn't paid to do so. He loved his life and said every day was a holiday!

Here are three amusing phrases Fritz quoted in *Scouse International* but was too happy and good natured to use in his own conversations:

Scouse – 'Yiv gorran ed as big as Bairkened'
English – 'You are more self-assured than is good for you'
French – 'Mets un peu d'eau dans ton vin'
German – 'Du bist total eingebildet'

* * * * * * * * * * * *

Scouse – 'Spissun down'
English – 'The rain is heavy today'
French – 'Il pleut des cordes'
German – 'Es giest'

* * * * * * * * * * * *

Scouse – 'T'rah wackh'
English – 'I'll bid you Good Day'
French – 'Au revoir'
German – 'Auf wiedersehen'

George Stephenson
1781–1848

The Rocket *at Rainhill*
The Liverpool & Manchester Railway

'Geordie' and 'randy' are two colloquial additions to the English language not usually attributed to the famous and highly revered locomotive pioneer. But it is George Stephenson, indeed, to whom we allegedly owe these previously unheard of expressions, as well, of course, as his more famous and immensely important contributions to the transport systems of this country and the world.

'Geordie', a mispronunciation of 'Georgie', was the family nickname for little George, born in the mining village of Wylam, about 8 miles outside Newcastle. The name 'Robert' also occurred regularly within the Stephenson family as George's father, George's brother and George's son each bore the name. All played a positive part in the full story of George's amazing achievements. Robert senior worked as a poorly paid, illiterate fireman at the Wylam colliery. He was, however, strong, dexterous and highly intelligent. He mended and adapted various pieces of equipment at the mine, bringing small items home to demonstrate to his children how these were constructed and how they operated. These pieces of machinery were, in fact, George's boyhood toys. No Meccano in those days (see Frank Hornby in *Liverpool's Own*), but the real thing, fully functional and serviceable.

Like other village children, George never went to school – no education was available. George started work at the age of eight, feeding and tending local horses and cows, but at home he was fascinated by his father's machines, taking them apart and learning the practicalities of how they worked. Later, as a young teenager, George worked in the local colliery, soon helping to solve many technical and engineering problems. Showing great self-motivation, George saved what little he could to pay for evening classes. He was determined to learn to read, write and calculate. At weekends, a well-read local farmer helped him in his quest for literacy and numeracy. George was forever grateful to him and when George eventually became rich and famous, he 'employed' his former tutor on the experimental farm attached to his elegant mansion.

While still an impoverished young man with a strident voice and a broad regional accent, George fell in love with Elizabeth Hindmarsh. Her father, owner of farming land and orchards, considered George their social inferior. The fact that George was handsome and highly ambitious carried no weight and Hindmarsh forbade any marriage. Elizabeth, deeply in love, claimed that if she could not wed George Stephenson, she would never accept anyone else. She kept her word although George eventually married Frances Henderson, nine years his senior. She gave birth to their two children, Robert and then Fanny but Fanny died almost immediately and Frances herself died the following year. George's sister cared for little Robert while George walked to Scotland in search of better employment.

On his return, always learning by practical experience rather than academic study, George experimented with many innovations. His earnings increased sufficiently for him to send Robert to good schools, where the boy made excellent progress. Robert shared his homework with his father, so George's education was greatly enhanced with the help of his son.

Trying to prevent the many fatal explosions down the mines, George designed a miner's lamp which he proved, in public, to be safe even in the advent of 'fire damp'. After a demonstration before an educated audience, the 'Geordie' Lamp, nicknamed after himself, was ready to be officially launched, when news arrived that Sir Humphrey Davy was about to present a similar lamp to the Royal Society. A huge argument ensued, with supporters on both sides claiming the original invention. Sir Humphrey won. George was enraged but was eventually proved to be the true innovator. However, even though compensation was paid, the damage was done – the 'Davy lamp' became more popular than the 'Geordie lamp'. George developed a hatred for classically educated rivals and his behaviour became brusque and impatient to the point of rudeness. Some say that it is after the Geordie lamp that folk from Newcastle earned their moniker.

In 1813/14, Stephenson was experimenting with the construction of a steam-powered locomotive that could pull a 30-ton weight at 4 miles per hour, far superior to anything that any team of horses could achieve. After a further sixteen prototypes, Stephenson's reputation began to spread. Even Elizabeth Hindmarsh's father was impressed. In 1820, George and Elizabeth were eventually allowed to wed, living happily together until Elizabeth's death in 1845. Elizabeth never had any children. Had they married sooner, Robert Stephenson would never have been born and George's education and thus career would have been seriously hampered.

With his teenage son, Robert, Stephenson surveyed the proposed railway line between Stockton and Darlington. This opened in 1825, with the *Locomotion* reaching speeds of 25 miles per hour and pulling 80 tons of coal. Father and son now worked in partnership. George's brother, another Robert, also joined the team, working on the management side of the business.

As rivals began to plan similar methods of transportation, a competition was devised, in 1829, to find the best locomotive to ply the planned Liverpool & Manchester Railway. Initially, there were ten potential entries but only five were ready in time. Of these, two withdrew with structural problems. The test involved travelling twenty times along a specially laid track at Rainhill. This replicated the return journey between Liverpool and Manchester. Pulling a load three times its own weight, the speed was set for at least 10 miles per hour. The trials, spanning three days, were widely publicised and became a hugely popular festive event, attended by the prime minister, the Duke of Wellington and many civic, political, industrial and engineering dignitaries. Fashionable ladies too, flocked to the 'carnival'. Ordinary folk were not debarred and crowds enjoyed the October spectacular. *Rocket*, designed and built by George and Robert Stephenson with assistance from George's brother and driven by Joseph Locke, proved superior to *Sans Pareil* and *Novelty*, winning the prize of £500.

In 1830, the Liverpool & Manchester Railway was officially opened by the Duke of Wellington, again attended by admiring crowds. Eight locomotives formed an impressive procession, each with elegant and high-ranking passengers. Nobody was used to such an exciting method of transport but when MP William Huskisson alighted from his carriage and crossed the track on foot, he was knocked down by the locomotive and seriously injured. Taken to hospital by George Stephenson, he died later that day.

In total, George Stephenson lived in Liverpool for three years. His excavations near Edge Hill criss-crossed above those of Joseph Williamson, the 'Mole of Edge Hill' (see *Liverpool's Own*). As Stephenson's labourers were delving into the sandstone bedrock, part of the sub-soil collapsed under them. Beneath, they were horrified to see Williamson's blackened and mud-spattered workers. The shock to each group was equally terrifying – Stephenson's team thought that they had dug right down to Hell while Williamson's men thought they were caught in an avalanche. Picks and shovels clattered onto the bedrock as every man turned tail and scattered, frightened out of their skins.

George and Robert each became widely fêted and in great demand, both in Britain and abroad. Their designs for bridges (locally, the 'skew' bridge at Rainhill station and the Britannia Bridge over the Menai Strait), railway lines and the standardisation of rail gauges were accepted and respected everywhere. They were consulted and handsomely rewarded in Europe and South America and their influence was acknowledged by contemporaries and successors including Joseph Locke and Isambard Kingdom Brunel. Father, son and brother worked sometimes together but increasingly independently, thus efficiency and output was doubled. Hundreds of new jobs were created, as more and more lines were laid and tunnels excavated. However, the lives of the navvies were hard and dangerous – everything had to be done by brute force or dynamite. There were no health and safety rules and navvies lived on site, in crude huts. They slept in their clothes, ate canteen stews or porridge and their frequent injuries were dealt with by bone setters and quacks. Brothels were set up nearby and on pay day, the men would drink ale and wander randomly to find a prostitute. This became known as going on a 'randie' or feeling 'randy'.

The advent of the railways brought enormous advantages to the country. Not only did passengers benefit, but the speedier transport of goods helped to vary the national diet and to expedite the transformation of raw imports such as cotton into textiles and clothing ready for export.

George ended his days at the Georgian-style mansion Tapton House, Chesterfield, having married his third wife Ellen Gregory only six months earlier. Robert, meanwhile, married Frances Sanderson in 1829 but they had no children. Both father and son were offered knighthoods, but both declined. From 1990 to 2003, British £5 notes carried an engraving of the *Rocket* with a portrait of George Stephenson on the reverse side.

Sir Henry Tate

1819–99

Sugar – Art – Philanthropy

The Lord Chamberlain
Is commanded by Her Majesty, Queen Victoria,
to offer Mr Henry Tate the title of Knight of the Garter and life Peerage of Baronet,
in recognition of his many generous donations to charitable and educational
establishments, over a long period of years, and for his services to British Industry, to
Commerce and to Art.
Buckingham Palace
Morning Dress Suit or Full Dress Uniform.
Her Majesty is privy to the fact that Mr Tate has already refused this honour upon
several previous occasions. Her Majesty and the Royal Family wish it to be known
that they will, however, be offended if he still feels unable to accept this most recent
invitation.
R.S.V.P.

The wording may have varied slightly but this, in essence, was the message received in 1898, by the ageing Henry Tate. This time he accepted and lived for one further year as the Baronet Sir Henry Tate. In 2001, a blue plaque was unveiled on the site of his first shop at 42 Hamilton Street, Birkenhead.

Born in 1819, in White Coppice near Chorley, Lancashire, Henry Tate was the son of a Unitarian minister. Henry's own education was basic and short. He left school at thirteen and was sent to Liverpool to take up an apprenticeship in a grocer's store. During the seven years of his very poorly paid training, he received instruction in stock control, accountancy and staff management. At the age of twenty he was freed from his indentures and immediately set up his own grocery business in Birkenhead. He was efficient, hard working and, a rarity in Victorian England, a caring and fair-minded employer. His success was rapid. By the time he reached thirty-five, he had built up a chain of six shops.

Importing sugar from America and the West Indies was then a thriving industry. Its history had been shameful in the days of the Trade Triangle where sugar, spices and raw cotton had been transported across the Atlantic from the New World to Britain. From there, manufactured goods were shipped to Africa while the cargo from Africa to America then consisted of kidnapped slaves destined to work in the cotton fields and sugar plantations of the West Indies and the United States. But due to Abolitionists such as Liverpool's William Roscoe, slavery had been illegal for fifty years before Tate set up his first business.

In 1841, Henry married Jane Wignall, who bore him eight children. In 1859, Henry became a partner in the firm of John Wright & Co. In 1861, he sold his grocery empire in order to concentrate solely upon sugar. When he bought out his partner in 1869, he changed the name from John Wright & Co. to Henry Tate & Sons. Initially, the huge blocks of sugar were heavy and difficult to handle. So in 1872, Henry bought a patent for making small sugar cubes from the German inventor, Eugen Langen. Henry set up a new

refinery in the aptly named Love Lane, Birkenhead. From then on, his rise to fame and fortune was meteoric. He leased offices in Chapel Street, Liverpool.

In 1885, the widowed Henry married again, to Amy Hislop. Now a millionaire (quite exceptional before the twentieth century), Henry did not use his fortune for personal luxuries – quite the opposite in fact. His lifestyle was unassuming without being miserly. Despite his lack of classical education, he found considerable enjoyment in the artistic works of his contemporary artists, especially the Pre-Raphaelites. He became friendly with John Everett Millais, who was only ten years his junior. Tate particularly admired Millais's study of Ophelia and the ever-popular 'Bubbles'. After amassing an impressive collection of British paintings, Henry adopted the custom of opening his own home to the public every Sunday, as a free art gallery. Eventually, he paid for a large new gallery to be built at

Millbank, near the Houses of Parliament. His only stipulation was that all paintings and sculptures must be by British artists.

Henry Tate's greatest delight was to make huge donations to a wide variety of charitable organisations. By nature modest and unassuming, he never courted publicity nor gratitude. Many of his gifts were anonymous, only being recognised after his death. Ever conscious of his own lack of further education, he focused on grants such as £42,000 for the founding of Liverpool University and £35,000 to Bedford College for Women (very forward-thinking and enlightened in the 1880s). Libraries in the downtrodden areas of Balham, Streatham, South Lambeth and Brixton all received generous funding from him, as did the Queen's Institute for District Nurses and the Hahnemann Homeopathic Hospital, Liverpool. Nor did he forget the Liverpool Royal Infirmary, which he helped to the tune of £5,000. The London-based (later Oxford-based) Manchester College received £15,000 to endow a new library and to encourage the 'theory and art of preaching and the continuing education of non-conformist students' in this Dissenting Academy. In 1889, Tate decided to donate his personal art collection to the nation, stipulating that the government should find or build a suitable gallery for such an exhibition. Thanks to his gift of £80,000, the National Gallery of British Art was opened in 1897, on the north bank of the Thames. In recognition of his benevolence, this museum has always been known as the Tate.

Although Abram Lyle was a contemporary of Tate's, living from 1820 to 1891, the two firms did not merge until after their deaths. Lyle's sugar business struggled for many years, making a loss of £30,000 in its first year. It was only when the famous tins of Golden Syrup appeared on the market that Lyle's fortunes rapidly improved. It was in 1921 that Henry's son, William, effected the merger to create Tate & Lyle. The sweet-toothed British soon coined the nickname 'Tate and Smile'. In the twentieth century the art galleries of Tate Britain and Tate Modern were joined by two other waterside Tate galleries. St Ives, Cornwall, famous for its exceptional sunshine and clear light, has long been a great favourite of painters and sculptors. Built on the site of a defunct gasworks, the state-of-the-art Tate Gallery and restaurant, overlooks one of St Ives' three superb beaches. Meanwhile, situated on the River Mersey, in a corner of the acclaimed tourist attraction, the Albert Dock, the Liverpool Tate now occupies the very warehouses where Henry Tate's sugar imports were once stored.

If ever there was a sweet life, it was that of Sir Henry Tate.

Mirabel Topham
1892–1980

Gaiety Girl – Grand National – Grand Prix – Grand Dame

Gaiety Girls were the WAGs of the late 1800s and early 1900s. They were beautiful, expensively fashionable and upwardly mobile. Their wardrobes were full of designer outfits from the very best couturiers. They, however, were also cultured, intelligent and decorous. George Edwards had coined the name because his musical shows were produced at the Gaiety Theatre in the West End of London. He chose his chorus line with great care, knowing that with such a tempting cast, he could attract audiences of very high social standing. 'Stage-door Johnnies' were often the heirs to a title or a fortune who were looking to improve their gene pool instead of inter-marrying within their own social circle. Indeed, many of George's girls were debutantes or 'blue-stockings' themselves. Many married into the aristocracy or into super-rich American dynasties. One became a Member of Parliament while several went on to distinguished careers in legitimate theatre. P.G. Wodehouse found inspiration for his *Blandings Castle* characters at the Gaiety Theatre.

One of the most remarkable of all the Gaiety Girls, the daughter of a successful publican, Mirabel's maiden name and her place of birth have slipped off the scoreboard. During her long and flourishing association with Merseyside, she was always known as Mrs Topham. Although not daintily pretty, when young she was impressively statuesque with a well-

Mirabel Topham with Stirling Moss at Aintree.

developed figure. As well as being an accomplished actress, singer and dancer, she also had great managerial and entrepreneurial potential. At that time, however, there were no opportunities for young women to forge a career in the world of commerce. Instead, she used her artistic talents rather than her intellectual abilities in order to make a living.

One of her admirers was Ronald Topham, sometimes known as Arthur. He was the grandson of Edward Topham who had succeeded William Lynn, the original creator of the Liverpool Grand Steeple Chase at Aintree. The land for the course had been leased from Lord Sefton. Young Ronald Topham had no interest in horses, jockeys, managing a racecourse or anything else except wine, women and song. After his marriage to Mirabel, he set up home in Warwickshire, intending to distance himself from Merseyside forever.

Mirabel had other ideas. She became fascinated with the developing enterprise. The equestrian thrills were only part of the appeal, however. It was the allure of the financial possibilities that engaged her imagination. She didn't bet at the Tote, she wanted more than just a flutter. Ronald put up no fences to her plans, he couldn't care less whether she succeeded or not. As long as he could drink the profits and gallop off to London whenever he chose, Mirabel could take over the reins completely. Which she did. She became everyone's favourite. Cool, clear-headed and always ahead of the field, her gamble paid off. By 1937, she was the Managing Director and Joint Secretary, remaining so for the next forty years. Her name and ebullient personality made her the emblem of the Grand National, as it had become. No other entries could match her pace nor stamina. There were difficult hurdles to overcome, fierce criticism of the injuries and deaths suffered by the horses, complaints about the noise and litter outside the grounds, punters invading the track, and abortive attempts to purchase the circuit from Lord Sefton before eventually persuading him to sell.

In spite of owning a townhouse in London's Regent Park, as time went by Mirabel hardly ever left the course. Within the grounds there was a tumbledown shack called Paddock Lodge. Mirabel had it rebuilt as her permanent home, giving it the nickname of Padlock Lodge. All her secrets and sadnesses were hidden from public view inside this cottage. Outwardly so admired and so fortunate, behind closed doors her marriage went lame. It was a non-starter, in fact. She and Ronald had no children and they were rumoured to sleep in separate rooms. Certainly, after a violent row, Mirabel took Ronald's niece, Pat into the master bedroom as protection. Ronald became an alcoholic and his behaviour in company and in public was an embarrassment. He was aggressive and destructive as well as childish and petty. He would switch off the lights while Mirabel was studying business papers and kick her pet dog. He was also jealous of non-existent suitors, although he was always lecherous with other women, often visiting shady ladies in London and at least once being convicted of indecent exposure in Regent's Park. Mirabel had to take out a court order to prevent the press from disclosing his misdemeanours.

Bur Mirabel was tough and far-seeing. She realised that a few race meetings per year were not enough to make a profit and Aintree Racecourse would cease to exist without a supplementary income. Mirabel went to visit the Duke of Richmond and Gordon, owner of the Goodwood Estate. Since 1948, motor racing had been added to the horse races there. The duke was the President of the British Automobile Racing Club and Mrs Topham was so impressed by the viability of this combination that she enlisted the duke's help in bringing motoring to Aintree. Once again, Lord Sefton tried to put up hurdles to the

enterprise but in 1952 a motor racing track was constructed to run parallel with the Grand National circuit. Stirling Moss was among the many famous drivers to be attracted to Aintree. He won his first Grand Prix there as well as on subsequent occasions.

Mirabel's personality, although amiable, became more and more controlling over the years. After Ronald's death, she persuaded his niece, Pat, and nephew, Jim, to come to live with her. Because she didn't want to lose their company, she plied them and all visitors with the most sumptuous of luxury foods. She also interfered with their love lives and broke up any tentative romances. She herself began comfort eating and the once-fit filly became an overweight mare, tipping the scales at 18 stones.

In old age, she took to her bed, claiming that she could concentrate so much better upstairs, using four telephones and keeping visitors at bay. Her favourite saying was, 'As I say to my staff, you do the doing. I do the thinking.' Even when the course was eventually sold to a property developer in 1973, the 'Topham Trio' still lived in Paddock Lodge. For years, the public was kept on tenterhooks with rumours of the demise of the now world-famous race but despite all the tumbles and stumbles, the Grand National has survived into the twenty-first century and now seems more popular than ever.

Robert Tressell (Robert Noonan)
1870–1911

Author of The Ragged Trousered Philanthropists

Frustration and fury seem to be the all-abiding motivation for the writing of one of the most widely read and frequently reprinted single novels of all time. An old, hard-backed copy, dated 1951, proudly proclaims, somewhat ungrammatically, on its cover, 'The complete unabridged edition 127th Thousand' [sic]. No author is accredited on the cover nor spine.

Inside, the reprints date from 1914 to 1951. By 2003, the book was estimated to have been reprinted over a hundred times and sold over a million copies. This does not take into account the fact that most copies are read by borrowers from libraries or passed down from one generation to another, thereby doubling or trebling these totals.

As well as being read all over the English-speaking world, there are translations into Russian, Japanese, Dutch, German and Bulgarian. It has also been the inspiration for many television, radio and stage adaptations, notably the 2010 production at the Liverpool Everyman Theatre and a commemorative drama event in 2011, at La Casa, Hope Street, and at the Liverpool Town Hall.

Robert Noonan adopted the pseudonym Robert Tressell in order to disguise his true identity, fearing reprisals from the employers and other figures of authority whom he caricatured in his novel. The theme depicts wretched working conditions and deplorable wages in the painting and decorating trade during the early years of the twentieth century.

Born in Ireland in 1870, Robert did not have the advantage of the classical education that his natural intelligence and many talents deserved. His father's early death left Robert with severe financial problems and, as for many promising youngsters of the time, further education was an unobtainable luxury. Robert, however, educated himself and was widely read in the classics, contemporary literature and political pamphlets.

As well as his gift for words and his artistic ability, Robert also took an active interest in the economical and political problems of the era. Frustrated at the lack of opportunities available in Ireland, he decided, in 1896, to emigrate to South Africa, hoping for a chance to better himself and possibly find relief from his constant chest infections. In South Africa, he married a local girl. Their only child, Kathleen, was born in 1892. A sad turn of fate caused Robert to be the lone custodian nurturing and providing for Kathleen. He was a caring and responsible parent, finding good schools, a nursemaid and domestic help for Kathleen. Father and daughter were devoted to each other and remained inseparable until just before his untimely death in 1911.

In 1901, when the threat of the Boer War became a reality, Robert brought Kathleen to Britain where they lived with one of his sisters, Adelaide, in Hastings. Adelaide was widowed, with a young son, Arthur, so both children benefited from the arrangement. But working as a painter/decorator/sign-writer, Robert rapidly became embittered by the injustice of the class system and the total disregard for the well-being of labourers shown by employers, clergy of all denominations and the MPs of all political parties. He joined various workers' groups and designed one of the huge banners to be carried in parades and demonstrations. Robert did not incite anarchy but he did attempt to influence his fellow artisans to stand up for their rights. He tried to highlight the financial iniquities of the wage systems of the time. Disheartened by the apathy he witnessed among his fellow craftsmen and furious at the duplicity, hypocrisy and rigid hierarchy within the employment system, Robert, weary, dismayed and physically weakened, would trudge home after a day that started at six and finished only when daylight failed. There he would continue with his labour of love, his novel.

Taking his cue from the works of Dickens, Robert caricatured his workmates and his bosses, inventing names that were almost onomatopoeic in their descriptiveness – Snatchum, Slyme, Councillor Didlum, Dr Weakling, Sweater, Grinder . . . the list goes on.

Mugsborough was his setting for the novel but everyone knows that it depicts the Hastings of that period. Tressell's main protagonist, Owen, surely autobiographical, rails against the compliance of his workmates, feeling that they are just as guilty as their bosses for the status quo. He wrote:

They were the enemy – those ragged trousered philanthropists who not only quietly submitted, like so many cattle to their miserable slavery for the benefit of others, but defended it, and opposed and ridiculed any suggestion of reform. They were the real oppressors – the men who spoke of themselves as 'the likes of us' who, having lived in poverty and degradation all their lives, considered that what had been good enough for them was good enough for the children they had been the means of bringing into existence.

Beth Tweddle MBE

From training fame to name of a train

Oscar Wilde's romantic hero in his famous play, *The Importance of Being Earnest* decides to invent a new name for himself, Bunbury. Beth Tweddle, who grew up in Bunbury, Cheshire, is a supreme example of the importance of being earnest, her dedication and zeal having earned her, to date, no less than ten gold medals, seven silvers and three bronze medals, in gymnastic championships all around the world.

In 1985, as her father was working in South Africa, Elizabeth Kimberly Tweddle was born in Johannesburg but only eighteen months later, the family returned to Britain. In spite of showing early promise as a gymnast, Beth recalls her initial reluctance to practice.

'When I first started gymnastics,' she explains, 'I wasn't a big fan of it in the slightest. In fact, I used to lock myself in my bedroom, so that I wouldn't have to go. After much persuasion and cajoling, I'd eventually be dropped off at the gymnasium. It was only when I got into the gym that I was fine. Then my parents couldn't get me off the premises again.

I'm not sure what it was. I think I was scared of being in a completely new environment. Only when I did my first competition did I realise that this was what I wanted to do. So I stopped crying every time I went to the gym!'

Beth's skill and artistry quickly became evident. In 1994, at the age of nine, she was accepted into the British Junior National Team. Three years later, while still a pupil at the Queen's School, Chester, she also enrolled at the Gymnastics Club in Toxteth, Liverpool. At the completion of her academic studies, Beth graduated from Liverpool John Moores University with a Sports Science Degree. She hopes that her future career may be as a physiotherapist.

Beth specialises in the discipline known as Uneven Bars, as well as in Floor Gymnastics. She has been a member of team events winning gold in Milan in 2009 and silver in Manchester in 2002. Her own gold medals were won in such far-flung venues as Rotterdam, London, Aarhus, Berlin, Birmingham (for both Bars and Floor) Milan (Bars and Floor) and Manchester, while her silvers were gained in Birmingham, Clermont-Ferrand, Amsterdam in 2004 (Bars and Floor) and again in 2007 and Manchester (Bars and All Round.) Add three bronzes in Patras, Anaheim and Melbourne and there can hardly be a more impressively decorated mantelpiece in the whole of Britain. The little girl who wouldn't leave her own bedroom has come a long way in a few short years.

Beth insists that she owes a great deal to her coach, Amanda Reddin, saying, 'Amanda has been the main influence in my career. She has been there through the highs of winning and the lows of disappointments and injuries. She knows exactly how to train me, to get the best out of me.'

Among so many highs, Beth counts 2006 as the best year of her career so far, adding:

This was the first year that I won major titles on a World and European level. Something that I had dreamed about but never thought I would achieve. I had Silver and Bronze medals but had never made it to the top of the rostrum. Strangely enough, the early part of the year started off pretty badly. I was named as team captain for the English troupe at the Commonwealth Championships but due to an ankle injury while training, I had to withdraw. This was particularly disappointing as I'd had to withdraw from the European Championships in 2005, again through injury, even after I'd qualified for all events. But then, after winning the European title in April 2006, the year just got better and better, winning my sixth National title and first World Cup title and then securing third place in the BBC Sports Personality of the Year. No other gymnasts have ever made the short list for this award.

Overall, Beth considers one of the highlights of her vocation to be winning the Commonwealth title in 2002, in Manchester.

This was my first major title, and it was in front of a home crowd and as close as I was ever going to get to competing in my home town of Chester. A lot of my family and friends were there for the event, whereas normally, at major championships it is usually just my parents. So it was really nice to be able to celebrate with everyone afterwards. Another special occasion was winning the World Title in 2006, on Bars, being the first British gymnast ever to win a world title. And I shan't forget 2009 in a hurry, either.

Winning World Title on Floor. This was in front of a home crowd in London. It had been a roller-coaster week. I had missed out on the Bars finals because I fell in qualification. But five days later I won Floor – especially rewarding as no-one expected me to win this.

Beth's achievements have been recognised in a variety of ways. In the New Year's Honours list of 2010, she was appointed Member of the Order of the British Empire. In September 2011, Beth leapt for joy at Lime Street station, Liverpool, at the launching ceremony of the Virgin train which is to carry her name the length and breadth of the country. She was delighted with the support this demonstrates for sports stars and athletes, especially as Virgin Trains will be assisting travel to training and championship events for young Olympic hopefuls. Beth has also been offered another potential occupation. When Team Visa were scouting for models to publicise a new range of high-octane designer outfits, they chose long-distance runner Mo Farah, teenage diver Tom Daley, paralympian riding champion Natasha Baker and our Beth. The beautiful coral evening dress by Marchesa was displayed to perfect advantage by Beth's graceful leaps and swirling dance steps. Co-designer Georgina Chapman went on record as saying, 'It was truly a pleasure to be working with Beth. Such strength and talent should always be applauded.'

Frankie Vaughan OBE CBE

1928–99

Francis Ephraim Abelson
Singer, dancer, philanthropist

Frankie Vaughan was the man who said, 'Thanks, but no thanks,' to Marilyn Monroe. Aged thirty-three, handsome and at the height of his popularity, our Frankie went to Hollywood to star in the romantic film *Let's Make Love* with that all-time icon of sexual desire, Norma-Jeane Mortenson, better known as Marilyn Monroe, and found himself on the receiving end of her flattering approaches. What red-blooded, attractive man could refuse what a president, a famous playwright and a boxing champion would all accept? Our Frankie, that's who! His firm reply was, 'I'm a very happily married man. My wife is my only lady.'

At the time that this happened, Frankie was a man of true morals and firm principles. He was a reformed character adhering to the values taught by his darling grandmother and his hardworking and conscientious grandfather and parents. But, as with many hot-headed youngsters, there had been a time in his life when he thought it was daring and clever to belong to a tearaway gang and to steal from poor but honest stall-holders in Liverpool's markets. Of course, it wasn't clever at all, market goods are on open display, no enclosed counters, no security devices; anyone can loot from such vulnerable citizens. Frankie soon came to realise this and to form a lifelong desire to help teenagers who might be tempted to follow in his foolish footsteps.

Frankie was the son of a Jewish family with high moral aspirations. His grandfather, born in Kiev was highly intelligent and multi-talented. He spoke five languages and had been employed by the British government as an interpreter during the Boer War. He'd also worked in the South African diamond mines. While Frankie was still a pupil at Prescot Street School and a choir boy at the Princes Road Synagogue, his grandmother would take her 'number vorn boy' (hence his showbiz name) on weekend trips to all the leisure spots and cultural centres of Merseyside. The bond between them was strong and affectionate and he owed many of his wider interests to her.

During the Second World War, evacuation took the family to Cumberland and Lancaster where Frankie enjoyed sports training at the Lancaster Boys' Club, playing football, table tennis and boxing. His talent as a singer was well matched by his artistic flair. At the tender age of fourteen, he won a scholarship to the Lancaster College of Art, with an exceptionally original study of the Liver Building as his presentation piece. Before his three-year course was completed, he was called up and served in the Royal Army Medical Corps for three years, stationed in Egypt and Malta, frequently entertaining the troops in musical shows. On leave, Frankie met and fell in love with Stella, a chemistry student. After a whirlwind romance of only three months, they wed in 1951, a lifelong marriage that was to bring them two sons and a daughter.

Back in Civvy Street Frankie assumed that art would provide him with a good career but when this didn't work out, he accepted an invitation from a theatrical agent, Billy Marsh, an acquaintance from his army days, to join a touring concert party. Here he met

the legendary Hetty King, a singer and male impersonator, a 'drag king'. Hetty, real name Winifred Emms, was born into a theatrical family in New Brighton, Wallasey. Dressed as an elegant military officer or a pipe-smoking sailor, her career spanned two world wars, entertaining troops. Between and after the wars, she played principal boy in panto or sang risqué songs dressed in top hat and tails. Married twice and hugely popular, she performed all over the country almost until her death in 1972. On meeting the young Frankie, she immediately saw his potential and took him under her wing, teaching him her high-kicking dance routine, sexy, swaggering saunter, and her over-the-shoulder glances with the suggestive raised eyebrow. Frankie's own natural charisma and friendly smile did the rest. The elegant top hat and tails outfit complemented his tall, slim figure very well and, in time he also added an equally dashing straw boater and Savile Row sports blazer. He quickly rose from supporting act to top of the bill. In Glasgow, he found some old Victorian sheet music of 'Give Me the Moonlight', which soon became his showpiece. This, with 'Kisses Sweeter than Wine', 'Garden of Eden', 'Pennies from Heaven' and 'Green Door' formed the core of his repertoire, making him a genuine matinée idol for female audiences everywhere. In 1956 he even joined a Dancing on Ice Show, 'Wildfire', learning to skate in only four weeks of intensive private lessons. His popularity was such that a recording career and television appearances, sponsored by Sir Bernard Delfont, were offered to him on a plate.

He came to the attention of the charming and popular film star Anna Neagle and her film director husband Herbert Wilcox. They cast Frankie in his first film, *These Dangerous Years*. One of the locations was the Merseyside promenade at Aigburth, Liverpool, known as the Cast Iron Shore, where the childhood Frankie had visited with his grandmother. Malta was another familiar location when they filmed *Wonderful Things*. Later came *The Lady is a Square*. The Hollywood films *Let's Make Love* and *The Right Approach* (when Marilyn made the wrong approach), came along in 1961. In 1973, Frankie, always a great football fan, led the singing of 'Abide With Me' and 'You'll Never Walk Alone' at the FA Cup final at Wembley.

Frankie had always been taught to be grateful for the good things in life, so now he wanted to put something back to acknowledge his good fortune. His Jewish faith was still very important to him, teaching as it does charity and support for others less fortunate. He had always devoted time to visit boys' clubs on his tours and now he invested even more time and donations to this worthy cause, eventually becoming vice-president of the National Association of Clubs for Young People. As his professional career slowed down, his charity work increased. He was highly regarded for his altruism, recognised in 1965 by an OBE. In 1988 he was awarded an Honorary Fellowship at Liverpool Polytechnic (now John Moores University) and in 1997 he received a CBE for services to Boys' Clubs.

After several heart operations, the man with the big heart and a wide smile died in 1999. His love for Merseysiders never waivered, being always full of admiration for their warmth and their tolerant good nature.

Derek John Harford Worlock
1920–96

The Most Reverend Derek Worlock, Archbishop of Liverpool

The titles of two of Derek Worlock's books, *Better Together* and *With Hope in our Hearts* exemplify his whole ethos. Even before his appointment as Archbishop of Liverpool, his pastoral and ecumenical works were of great importance to him. He was a man of the people with a deep understanding of the needs and emotions of his friends and parishioners. This was typified by his close association with David Sheppard, Anglican Bishop of Liverpool. Their first book, *Better Together*, was a joint enterprise and their *With Hope in our Hearts* echoes the lyrics of Liverpool FC's football anthem, 'Walk on, walk on, with hope in your heart.'

As the two bishops were as close as the fictional twins in *Alice in Wonderland* by Lewis Carroll, one of their many affectionate nicknames was 'Tweedledum and Tweedledee'. Derek and his twin sister were actually born in Marylebone, London, in 1920, in a flat overlooking Lord's Cricket Ground. Their parents, Captain Harford Worlock and Dora Worlock, (née Hoblyn, a women's rights activist) already had one son who eventually gave his life at sea during the Second World War. Derek's father was descended from a long line of Protestant clergymen but Derek's parents both converted to Catholicism. Such was their devotion that, from the age of three, little Derek never wavered from his own aspirations to become a priest.

From 1934 to 1944, while the family were living in Winchester, Derek studied at St Edmund's College. His academic work was always most meticulous, an admirable trait serving him well later in life, as he never entered any conference or meeting unless he had every detail at his fingertips.

He was ordained in Westminster Cathedral in 1944, exempting him from National Service unless needed as a military chaplain. Serving in Kensington, London, however, he experienced the devastation of the wartime air raids, especially the notorious 'doodle-bugs'. He later recalled that, sadly, he had administered the last rites to more than fifty bomb victims before encountering a single death from natural causes. After the end of the war, the Revd Worlock spent nineteen years as secretary to the Cardinals Griffin, Godfrey and finally Heenan. In 1965, he was appointed Bishop of Portsmouth. Here he began his efforts in improving ecumenical relationships with other Christian denominations, as well as renewing parishes and creating over thirty new church buildings. Derek always felt ill-at-ease during the years when Catholic and Protestant friends were forbidden to attend weddings, funerals or any other services in the churches of other denominations. A delicate situation arose when the daughter of a neighbouring Anglican bishop decided to marry her Catholic fiancé. Derek devised the perfect solution, presiding over the spiritual blessing on the morning of the wedding, while the bride's father performed the nuptial ceremony in the afternoon.

It was of particular pleasure to Derek that before his appointment as Archbishop of Liverpool in 1976, his 'opposite number' David Sheppard, already Anglican Bishop of Liverpool, had been consulted by the Catholic Archbishop, Bruno Heim, regarding the pastoral concerns in such a cosmopolitan area as Merseyside. It was after this amicable discussion that Derek Worlock was judged to be the most suitable candidate. Derek and David had already been neighbours in London, when Derek's work took him to the Stepney Dock area and David was attached to the Mayflower Family Centre, Camden Town.

The modernistic concrete, conical structure of the Metropolitan Cathedral of Christ the King, standing at the crown of Mount Pleasant, Liverpool, quickly earned it the comical nickname of 'Paddy's Wigwam' and 'The Pope's Rocket'. Derek embraced both with his usual warmth and humour. As he was not a born and bred Scouser, his southern accent was the butt of many jokes and imitations, prompting one old Merseysider to accuse him of sounding 'like the bloody Duke of Edinburgh!' Derek always accepted this with natural good humour.

During his tenure of office, however, Merseyside experienced tragedy, civil unrest, severe unemployment and corruption in local government. Derek and David showed practical and intuitive sympathy for the grief caused by the terrible losses at Hillsborough. They worked constantly with the leaders of the Baptists, Methodists, United Reformed Church and Salvation Army to offer as much comfort as possible to the distraught families. After the Toxteth riots of 1981, both strove to bring about solutions to the problems of disenchantment and to create a better sense of community spirit. Their genuine affinity and down-to-earth determination helped to ensure that Merseyside renounced old factions from the days of 'Orange versus Green'. They set the perfect example of non-sectarianism in their multicultural city.

Archbishop Worlock was efficient and methodical in all he did. His excellent memory and instinctive humanity were supplemented by his copious notes and an audio diary dictated every night before retiring to bed. In spite of an operation for lung cancer in 1992, he was well enough to celebrate the Golden Jubilee of his priesthood in 1994. It was also in 1994 that he and Bishop David Sheppard were granted the Freedom of the City of Liverpool and, when the New Year's Honours were announced, Derek was awarded the

Archbishop Derek Worlock (right) and Bishop David Sheppard.

Companion of Honour. Sadly, before the actual investiture, his condition worsened and he passed away a week before he was due at Buckingham Palace.

The matching statues of Father James Nugent and Canon Major Lester, devoted friends and colleagues during the dark days of Liverpool's nineteenth century, stand several metres apart in St John's Gardens, behind St George's Hall (see *Liverpool's Own*). The joint memorial sculpture to the twentieth-century Archbishop Derek Worlock and Bishop David Sheppard, demonstrates their closeness passing through a metaphorical doorway to heaven, in Hope Street which joins their two cathedrals.

David Yates

The road to Platform 9¾
Director of four Harry Potter films

How does a young Merseysider get to meet J.K. Rowling, Daniel Radcliffe, Rupert Grint, Emma Watson and a multitude of other world-famous film and television stars? One sure way is by becoming a genius at film directing – and genius, according to Thomas Edison, is 'one per cent inspiration and ninety-nine per cent perspiration.' Meaning, of course, that talent is important but hard work and determination are even more essential.

Take, for example, David Yates, born in St Helens and brought up in Rainhill, Merseyside. His start in life was an unhappy one, as both his parents died when he was still very young. He had already shown an interest in television and cinema – not just as a passive leisure activity for himself, but in the creative process of writing, directing and filming, as a medium for the entertainment of audiences far and wide. While other youngsters were interested only in the stars on the screen, David had been impressed by the directing skills of David Lean, Ken Loach and Martin Scorsese. His mother had recognised this and had bought him a Super 8mm camera as a present, something he treasured after her death. He used it to record friends and family and to produce a short film called *The Ghost Ship*, shot on location aboard the boat where his uncle was working as a cook.

David Yates directing on the set of one of the Harry Potter *films.*

After good results at school, David became a student at St Helens College, where he studied Sociology, Politics and Literature. Following this, he went to the University of Essex and then, from 1984 to 1987, to Georgetown University in Washington DC. Back in Britain, he joined the Cre8 Studio in Swindon and made his first main film, *When I was a Girl*, shot in and around Swindon. At the San Francisco International Film Festival, this won the award for the best short film. David then went to the National Film and Television School in 1989. While he was still a student there, the powers that be at the BBC engaged him to direct *Oranges and Lemons*. One of his early successes was *The Weaver's Wife*, a dramatic short, filmed during 1994 and 1995. Moving into mainstream television, David directed several episodes of *The Bill* and made a documentary about Brighton, Eastbourne and Weymouth, called *A Tale of Three Seaside Towns*. Stephen Fry and Robert Hardy starred in David's production of *The Tichborne Claimant*, filming several scenes on Merseyside and on the Isle of Man. This won many plaudits at the Edinburgh International Film Festival. The next step on David's route to international acclaim came in 2000 when he directed fellow Merseysider Pete Postlethwaite in *The Sins*, and John Suchet in the serialised adaptation of *The Way We Live Now*. In 2002, jointly with Andrew Davis, David Yates won the BAFTA for Best Drama.

When Daisy Ashford was only nine years old, she wrote a novel entitled *The Young Visiters* [sic] the story of an ungainly middle-aged man who seeks instruction from an aristocrat, as he needs to improve his knowledge of polite etiquette to impress an up-market lady. Jim Broadbent and Hugh Laurie starred in David's television adaptation of this little gem. In stark contrast, David's next project was *Sex Traffic*, a delicate depiction of a shocking subject. Different again, David enjoyed working with Jude Law and Bill Nighy, when he directed Richard Curtis's screen play, *The Girl in the Café*.

While taking a break in Cornwall from the remake of *Brideshead Revisited*, David received a call inviting him to direct the fifth *Harry Potter* film. As he had never read the any of the books nor undertaken anything similar to this form of cinematography, David invited his predecessor, Mike Newell, out for a drink to learn more about this new and somewhat daunting project. In fact, the very first scene David had to direct involved a giant interacting with human actors. This was the first high-scale visual effects item David had ever attempted in his life. The finished article attracted rave reviews and enormous box-office success. So much so, that David continued to direct all four of the remaining *Harry Potter* films. In total, he worked for six consecutive years on the J.K. Rowling saga, from 2006 to 2011. *Harry Potter and the Deathly Hollows* parts one and two, were filmed back to back and were praised for their 'dark' atmosphere and 'uncondescending sympathy' for Rowling's characters, as well as for their loyalty to source material. Part two was released in 2011 to universal acclaim and record-breaking commercial success.

Standing in the great hall during *Harry Potter and the Order of the Phoenix*, David suddenly realised, 'My God – this all started in St Helens! As a schoolboy I never imagined any of this. Back then I was just thinking about telling a story, which is what all young film-makers should be doing today.'

Is it the lavish CGI-enhanced 3D special effects or the depth of the characterisations that draw the crowds in countries all over the world?

'There are many reasons,' says David. 'J.K. Rowling has given us so many vivid characters. And there's a sense of wish fulfilment. There's the fight between good and evil, the power of love and faith as well as a sense of loss and dealing with loss.'

Not only did David master the secrets and technical wizardry of the special effects, he became the esteemed blue-eyed boy of the author and all the cast and crew. J.K. Rowling says, 'Everyone who watches part two will see that David Yates has steered us home magnificently. It's incredible.'

Daniel Radcliffe says, 'David added his own sense of grit and realism to the *Harry Potter* films. I think we all had a fantastic time working with him. I know I did.'

Bill Nighy calls David 'A quiet genius,' and Rhys Ifans describes his directing skills as being genuinely child-like in his obvious pleasure and enjoyment, saying, 'When he's pleased, he says "Fabby!" When he's happy, he jumps up and down. And when he's ecstatic, he skips all over the place!'

Six billion dollars says that he has every right to be ecstatic – all the hard work and long years of study were worth it. Now ready to move on, with other films already in production, David looks back with affection.

'I'm going to miss the people involved,' he says. 'We've had a tremendous family, both behind and in front of the camera. There's something unique between us. We've all been to the moon together. It's been a wonderful experience.'

Acknowledgements

As with my previous book, *Liverpool's Own*, I honour the memory of three brilliant people without whom no literary work of mine could ever have been possible. My debt to their talents and dedication is boundless. They are Mr Charles Babbage (1779–1869), Mr Peter Mark Roget (1791–1871) and Mr Oxford Concise!

My sincere thanks go to my editor at The History Press, Michelle Tilling, whose kind support, patience and understanding have been of the utmost importance to the successful conclusion of this and my previous book and recently also Richard Leatherdale. Eileen Brewer, as always, is the person to whom I turn for her IT skills, so superior to my own. Her invaluable help at any time of the day is matched only by her tolerance and unfailing good nature.

For technological support over and above the call of friendship, especially in respect of photography and electronic images, no-one could have been more helpful and constantly amiable than Dougie Redman, Runcorn's gift to Merseyside.

For unfailing support in literary and content references plus suggestions for topics, I am forever grateful to John Goldsmith MD, FRCP; Nan McKean BA (Hons); Bill McKean RD, MB, ChB, FRCGP; Geoff Woodcock BA, MA, PhD, FRA; and Jenny Woodcock BA, PhD, FR (Scot). Also to John Frodsham, Assistant Principal at St Helens College, Tim Bolton and Francesca Garner at Hugh Baird College, Hannah Longworth at Pilkington's World of Glass, Tony Hall at the *Liverpool Echo*, Sophie Callender – PA to Beth Tweddle, Fiona Whitfield at the Lancashire Wildlife Trust, William (Billy) Dean at the Liverpool School of Tropical Medicine, Sharon Ruddock at L.A. Productions, Professor Paul Baines – Head of School of English at Liverpool University, Nathan Pendlebury at the National Museums and Art Galleries Merseyside and all the receptionists and curators at the Chambré Hardman House, National Trust, 59 Rodney Street, Liverpool.

To all the present-day celebrities and their agents and P.A.S., I also send my sincere appreciation and good wishes for their continued success, as our wonderful ambassadors for Merseyside.